The
Procrastinating
Child

☼

ALSO BY RITA EMMETT

The Procrastinator's Handbook

The Procrastinating Child

A HANDBOOK FOR ADULTS
TO HELP CHILDREN
STOP PUTTING THINGS OFF

~~~~~~~~~~

Rita Emmett

Walker & Company
New York

First published in the United States of America in 2002
by Walker Publishing Company, Inc.

For information about permission to reproduce selections
from this book, write to Permissions, Walker & Company,
435 Hudson Street, New York, New York 10014

Library of Congress Cataloging-in-Publication Data

Emmett, Rita.
The procrastinating child : a handbook for adults to help children
stop putting things off / Rita Emmett.
p. cm.
ISBN 0-8027-7636-1 (pbk. : alk. paper)
1. Procrastination. 2. Children—Time management. 3. Teenagers—
Time management. 4. Child rearing. I. Title.

BF637.P76 E475 2002
649'.64—dc21   2002071376

Visit Walker & Company's Web site at www.walkerbooks.com

Printed in Canada

2   4   6   8   10   9   7   5   3   1

Dedication

This book is dedicated to those who hold the future of the world in their hands—children, including our grandchildren, Ken, Mike, Kortenay, Meghan, Connor, Cassidy, Noah, Kailey Jean, and Brynn.

And to those who love children—to parents and to anyone else who has ever reached out to help a child, including those of you who have never had or raised a child, but still care about them and offer a hand to them on occasion. This is a better world because of all of you.

Contents

Acknowledgments and Appreciation

Many people traveled along the path with me on the journey of creating this book. I humbly learned it would have been a long and miserable road to travel alone, and I am so grateful to every one of them for their support and encouragement. There are too many names to list here, but I smile just thinking of you. And the thought of some of you out-and-out makes me laugh.

Thank you to my colleagues, friends, and family for cheering me on. My heartfelt thanks to all those who shared their procrastination stories with me. Some were sad, some funny, some enlightening, and some poignant, but all helped to make this book richer and more relevant. When people read this and say to themselves, "Wow, this sounds just like our family" it is because of all the insightful stories you have added to this collection.

Special thanks to the "magnificent seven readers" who patiently plowed through the rough, rough draft—Nora Bennett, Kym Karder, Debra Kimbrough, Jo-Anne Knight, Pete Walkey, Maureen Edgar, and Curt Hansen; and special thanks to Sandra Baumgardner, of DuPage County (Illinois) Health Department, for her guidance when I couldn't figure out which way to turn.

My sincere appreciation to Mark Victor Hansen and Dottie Walters for their help and advice in learning about the world of books, and to the world's best and most patient literary agent, Jane Jordan Browne, who is not only hardworking, wise, and funny but also willing to explain and reexplain contracts to me, and who apparently believes that some day I will understand them. She also is the first person who believed my book might be worth publishing.

Everyone at Walker & Company feels like family to us. I am enormously grateful to two special people in particular: publisher George Gibson constantly astonishes me with how he goes beyond my hopes and expectations in the stellar support he gives my books. His creativity and vision bring joy to my heart. And my editor, Jackie Johnson, is brilliant in all she did to transform this book into what it is today. I love brainstorming with both of you, and am grateful to all the Walker gang for the standard of excellence in every detail and every aspect of our work.

My family has been eternally patient during those times I seem to drop off the face of the earth and lock myself in the office. Instead of getting cranky, they ask about the book, offer ideas, cheer me on, and fill my life with so much happiness— especially the wind beneath my wings, my husband, Bruce. People who know him ask me, "Has he STILL not read anything you've written?" He hasn't, but he's a great guy and is my *anam cara,* my soul friend. Traveling life's journey with him is a comfort and delight, and always, always full of surprises.

Each of you has been a blessing in my life, and because of all of you, it has been a wonder-full, joy-full journey. How could I be so lucky? Thank you and God bless you all.

The
Procrastinating
Child

✵

Introduction

~~~~~~~

WHEN CHILDREN WHO PROCRASTINATE are asked, "Why don't you just do it when you're supposed to?" invariably the answer is, "I don't know." Children, including teens, do not have the vocabulary, the insight, or the understanding to explain to us why they procrastinate.

As a professional speaker who presents keynotes and seminars, including "Improve Parenting Skills" and "Strategies to Blast Away Procrastination," I recently took a survey of adults who procrastinated as children. Over and over the same answer kept popping up: "There may be many reasons why I procrastinated as a child, but for me it was because nobody taught me any other way to do things, and so I simply put off doing everything."

Robert, an adult who was a great procrastinator as a child, explained that when he brought home low grades on his homework, his parents tried to "motivate" him by yelling and telling him that he was smart and capable of earning A's and B's. Then they sent him off to do his homework. But he remembers constantly feeling overwhelmed by all the homework he had to do; he didn't know where to start or how to break it down and do one step at a time.

Catherine wrote a similar story of how her military father would be in a fury over her messy room and would not allow her to go out till she cleaned it. She would stand in the middle of her room feeling helpless and hopeless. So she would pick up a dirty sock, then a blouse that needed to be hung up, then a wad of crumpled paper, then a catcher's mitt, and she'd stand there holding all these items and start to cry because she didn't know what to do next.

Any adult—not just a parent—can decide to help a child stop procrastinating. Teachers spend a tremendous amount of their time and energy on procrastinating students. Grandparents, other family members, friends, or neighbors who may be raising or helping to raise children, or giving day care, are also impacted by the despair of dealing with procrastinating kids.

However, you may not be aware of the high price children pay for procrastination in terms of their self-esteem and confidence. They consider themselves losers or feel like giving up. They are often punished by their parents or by school authorities (or both), and may be teased or ridiculed. Children can become downtrodden or depressed because of their procrastination. And there is no question that procrastination keeps a child from fully accomplishing short-term and long-term goals.

When are children procrastinating and when are they simply acting like children? It's normal to occasionally have to remind them to get themselves ready, feed the pet, or do their chores and homework on time. As frustrating as it is to remind the child, if it's only occasional and if the child does what she is supposed to do after being reminded, procrastination is not a serious problem. But children are considered to be procrastinators if they frequently need to be reminded, yet they still don't do what they are supposed to do or they finally do it only after a nightmare of tears, arguments, or some other kind of emotional upheaval.

There is no certain age that is the best time to help a child stop procrastinating. The problems and solutions are remarkably similar for children of all ages; it's the intensity that varies from child to child, from age to age. The five-year-old who dawdles getting ready for school in the morning or the teenager who can't get started on his homework are both wrestling with the same kinds of issues (being unmotivated, feeling overwhelmed, not knowing where to start, and—sometimes—taking great delight in pushing some adult's "anger button"), and both respond to similar solutions.

How This Book Will Help

This book is not set up according to specific procrastination problems (homework, chores, getting ready for something, taking care of pets), because for both children and adults, a procrastination problem usually involves a mixture of reasons, causes, and solutions.

For example, the teen who puts off sending in his college application might procrastinate because it has become a habit (chapter 1). Or he may not have learned any self-motivating skills (chapter 2); he may feel overwhelmed by all the papers to fill out (chapter 3); he may hate this type of task (chapter 4); or he may feel he doesn't have time (chapter 5). He may be waiting for a whole day free of interruptions so he can do it perfectly (chapter 6), or have some fears and anxieties about going away to college (chapter 7). He might not know where all the forms are because they are scattered all over his desk, bedroom, and locker (chapter 8), and he may be so swamped with other activities that he can't focus on this task (chapter 9).

The book addresses general areas of a child's life and explores reasons children put things off. Specific solutions are given for a wide variety of procrastination problems. In several of the chapters, solutions for you to share with the child are summarized in an acronym, with the first letter of each step spelling out a word. You might want to write these out and post them where the child can easily see them, or communicate them to the child verbally. Some of these concepts could be the springboard to conversations that bring you and the child closer.

Children Hate Having Ideas Forced on Them

No matter how long it has been since you were a child, no doubt you clearly remember that the more someone shoved an idea at you, the harder you shoved back. We just can't go galloping up to a child, shouting, "You're broke, and I'm going to fix you. Sit down and listen."

Forcing anything on a child usually results in arguments, resentment, and rebellion. Instead you will develop techniques to open lines of communication in a helpful, positive, loving way, and not be dictatorial. The aim is not to be too controlling or permissive—but simply to be firm and kind. Kindness shows respect for the child, and firmness shows respect for what needs to be done.

Timing is also important. If your child is resistant to working on her procrastination, she is likely to be more open to changing when she:

- is discouraged about not being able to get things done;
- has suffered some consequence of putting off a job and realizes that if she had done whatever it was earlier, her life would have been much better or happier; or
- is overwhelmed with too much to do and recognizes that she needs help.

These are ideal times to start talking to her about some of these concepts. If you force these principles and techniques on a child, you not only will meet with resistance and possibly rebellion, but you will fail to help her develop any initiative, organizational skills, or planning skills.

No Single Theory or Technique Works for Every Child

If you've had any experience with more than one child, you know how a toy or a book might enthrall one child for hours, yet bore the other one to tears. You might run something past two children, and one has a lightbulb flash over her head while the other stands there blinking at you as if you were talking some interplanetary language.

Whenever I present seminars on improving parenting skills, the subject of what to do about procrastinating kids arises. Frequently some parents in the seminar have read several books on parenting skills, so I survey them and ask if anyone has come across any books that specifically focus on how to help children stop procrastinating. No one has come up with any yet. I suspect the reason is because it is hard to motivate kids and guide them through the process of changing their attitudes and behavior. One brilliant idea simply will not work for all of them. There is no "quick fix," and there are no guarantees for what works with children. Although this book will offer help, there is no guarantee that it will work for every child.

On the other hand, one dad in a seminar told me that as he works to help his three daughters blast away their procrastination, he is observing tremendous improvement in their self-esteem and self-confidence. This is an exciting "extra" that goes along with helping our children stop procrastinating; research shows that poor self-esteem is frequently one of the major causes of teens choosing a troubled path in life.

Children Don't Always Think and Act the Same Way You Do

Let's be honest. Children hardly ever think and act as we do. You might prefer to work in profound silence; your offspring might actually have more success completing homework with loud music blaring. You might prefer doing chores at the end of the day; your child prefers waking up early to complete chores. You might believe that the first thing they need to do when they come home from school is start their homework, but your high-energy youngsters might need to run around and blow off steam for thirty minutes or so before settling down to schoolwork. One child might complete all schoolwork, or chores, or pet care, before dinner, while the other works best after dinner.

As you talk with children, do some brainstorming to help them figure out their best time and "style". Letting them make some of these decisions will help them work *with* you, not *against* you.

Of course, if they do their work at their choice of time and circumstances, and the work is completed and well done, no matter how weird their choice is, you have to admit that it works. But if the work is not complete or well done, then the deal's off, and they do it your way.

EXPECT OBSTACLES

Yes, there will be obstacles to your guiding your children toward accepting these ideas.

- They may resent any discussion about changing their habits.
- If they are teens, they may simply resent any discussion. Period.
- It may be hard to get them to sit still.
- They may have the attention span of a flashbulb. Poof. It's over.
- Children are definitely not interested in self-improvement.
- They may not understand the ideas.
- They are not open to anything you have to say.
- You don't have any confidence in yourself, and the whole idea of communicating to your child about procrastination creeps you out.

You're not alone, and you're not weird. All parents have these concerns. Even parents who are professional teachers feel intimidated about presenting to their own children these concepts about how to stop procrastinating. And if nobody taught you these principles when you were little, you have no role model, no example. Relax. As you read the stories of other parents, you'll probably find yourself saying, "Wow, that's just like my child," or "That sounds exactly like our family!"

Once you and your child begin communicating openly about procrastination, your child might ask a question that you don't know the answer to. That's okay. You don't have to *be* perfect, and you don't have to *act* perfect in front of your child. Nobody in this world has all the answers.

THE BIG QUESTION

Are you now—or have you ever been—a procrastinator? If yes, that's good. Why is it good? If you are or have been a procrastinator, then you can fully understand how your procrastinating child feels—overwhelmed, distracted, hopeless. And if you are now a procrastinator, you can work together with your child in changing *your* putting-off habit. You can practice ideas from this book and share these ideas with your children. Tell them about your successes, what works for you; tell them about your failures, what is hard and what does NOT work for you.

This might be a whole new level of communication for you and your children. Our offspring take great delight in hearing us tell about our mistakes and failures; this kind of conversation might actually create a closer bond between you and them.

A recent survey requested advice for parents of procrastinating children. This is what Helena wrote: "My advice is to fix your own procrastination habits, so you can lead your children by example. When you accomplish something on time, and have done it well, tell your children about it! Let them see you feeling proud that your projects are completed before the deadline. Talk to them about how important it is to live now, not 'tomorrow.' This is a precious gift we can give to our children."

Forming a Team

As you absorb the concepts in this book and decide to communicate them to your child, you don't have to create a teacher-student relationship, and you won't have to preach. You and the child are forming a team. Sometimes you will be the coach, giving guidance and encouragement, and once in a while you might send up a cheer or a pat on the back. Sometimes you will work as equal partners, brainstorming a problem or simply telling a story of your own struggle with the same type of situation. Sometimes you and your child might even have fun discussing one of the ideas.

You will come across short, quick, easy steps in sidebars labeled "Tips to Share with Your Child." You may decide to cover each section as you come to it, or take one chapter each week or each month or every so often. When you come to the "Tips" section, you might be thinking, Ah, I know exactly how I'm going to handle this. Other times, you might be stumped.

In that case, at the end of each chapter, there will be a "Teamwork" section for you to fill in for yourself about "Ideas to Discuss" with your child and some "Ideas in Action." You'll notice that this section will summarize the chapter, so you can check off the chapter's concepts and actions you want to cover, and there is room for you to write in your own ideas.

What's the difference between "discussion ideas" and "action ideas"? For example, under the "Discussion" section, you might want to cover what is in the chapter, but you also might want to discuss a character in a TV show that you and your child recently watched, and point out how that character created the problem by putting off a decision or action.

Or you might simply ask her what the word *procrastination* means to her.

In the "Action" section, you might check off an idea or two from the book, but then you might write something unique to you and that child, for example:

- "Offer to drive to activities more often so we have time to chat."
- If the child is in primary grades or younger: "Make macaroni necklaces with her, and tell her the story of Beth."
- If he is in middle school: "Pull out the jigsaw puzzle that he loves and work on it with him. Bring up the subject of perfectionism."
- For a teenager: "Let her invite Traci over to make taco salads, and while we are all chopping, tell them about my success using a kitchen timer this week."

One suggestion that applies to children of all ages: Pay attention to the whole relationship. You don't want to sacrifice the child's self-esteem or your friendship with her because you want her to do things your way. You'll get lots of ideas in this book. There's likely to be one or more that will make a big difference to your child. Relax and enjoy the journey. You may find that some of the discussions this book generates might even result in a closer relationship. As a bonus, that child will be learning skills that will help her function in a much more happy and successful way as an adult, both professionally and personally.

1

~~~~

Why Do Children Procrastinate?

CHILDREN OF ALL AGES, NATIONALITIES, and races are repeatedly asked by exasperated adults, "Why didn't you do it when you were supposed to?"

Wouldn't it be refreshing if just once the child gave an honest reply, such as, "I procrastinated"? More often than not, the adults become even more exasperated by the variety of excuses they receive:

"Welllllll, the computer ate my homework."

"I didn't have time."

"I dunno."

"It's too hard."

"I don't know how."

"I don't get it."

"You just don't understand."

"No, really, you never believe me. The computer really did eat my homework!"

Or from younger children they hear:

"My brother made me go outside and play."

"Well, you see, this big monster came along, and then, and

then he made a mess, and then he threw stuff all over the room, and then, and then he went away."

"I was afraid."

"My sister wouldn't let me."

Children put off the nuttiest things for the nuttiest reasons. Sometimes they spend more time giving us excuses than it would have taken to do the job itself. They make themselves crazy. They make parents crazy. They make teachers crazy. They make caregivers crazy. They make their families crazy.

Well, there is hope, and there is help. I was born the world's greatest procrastinator. My mother claimed that she was pregnant for ten months with me—I actually put off being born for a month. My homework was perpetually late, my chores were constantly forgotten, our poor pets (which I always promised to care for) would have starved if my family hadn't bailed me out, and whenever it was time to get ready for anything—going to school, going to bed, taking a bath, visiting relatives—I would put it off until my parents got hoarse yelling, "Now! Do it now!"

I felt that everything was out of my control, that I couldn't help the way I was; I believed that I never fit very well in this world, and that many significant people (including teachers, Scout leaders, and my family) didn't like me because I was never doing what I was supposed to be doing.

I didn't want to constantly put things off; I didn't want to lie when I forgot to do something; I just didn't know any other way to be. I didn't even *know* there was another way to do things. Some people did things on time, but I thought they were born with something special about them that I just wasn't lucky enough to have.

Then, after I grew up, I converted. I'm now a recovering procrastinator. Organized. Effective. Functional. Very happy.

In a study by the National Institute of Education, in which 1,000 thirty-year-olds were asked if they felt their high school education had equipped them with the skills they needed for the real world, over 80 percent responded, "Absolutely not." So this is your chance to teach your child one skill that most schools never have time to teach—how to stop procrastinating.

If a child has a procrastination problem, this book is here to help you help that child. Some people think a five-year-old procrastinates by crying, where a seventeen-year-old might procrastinate by storming out of the house. No, they procrastinate by putting things off. The crying or storming out is a result of communication problems, stress, anxiety, rebellion, or relationship difficulties within or outside the family. It's not our goal here to address those issues; the goal of this book is to help your child stop putting off what he should be doing.

RULES TO PREVENT PROCRASTINATION

The first step is, if you are in charge of the house rules or of any rules that could impact this child's life, establish rules now that support doing chores and tasks right away, and not putting them off. For example:

- Do homework first, then TV.
- Do chores first; then you can go on the computer.
- If you take too long getting ready in the morning, then you have to go to bed earlier at night.
- Put away jacket, shoes, backpack, and school things before doing whatever it is you like to do when you first come home from school (snack, call a friend, collapse in front of the TV).

These examples apply to children of all ages, but an example of specific rules for teens might be:

- Get good grades, and you can occasionally use the family car; bad grades equal no car for that semester.

These types of rules not only support children and help them to "do it now," they also establish good habits and break the frustrating habit of procrastination. Of course, your rules have to reflect your family's values.

It's Simply a Habit

So let's start there. Often procrastinating children believe that they were born with something missing. They believe they were born putting things off, that it's part of their personality, and that they can never change. They feel helpless and hopeless about the situation and about themselves. In addition, when children hear some adult refer to them as procrastinators, they believe it and then continue to behave accordingly.

Whether you are a procrastinator or not, when you start this process with a child, it's your job to let him know that procrastination is neither a personality trait nor a character flaw. It is simply a habit, and we can all change our habits.

If they have witnessed another child changing a habit, discuss that with them.

- Alberto and his friend Noah used to fight when they were four-year-olds because Noah would never help Alberto pick up his toys when they were finished playing, but now, one year later, Noah has changed and cooperates in cleaning up.

- Eleven-year old Corey has a friend who was always getting into trouble for talking in school, and now that friend has learned to control the chatter.
- Robin, a high school freshman, told of how impressed she was with a classmate who in eighth grade bragged that she never studied or completed assignments; now that classmate has become a good student who has developed terrific study habits.

Most of us don't know the reasons people change, but we all know someone who has stopped or started a habit.

If you've ever quit smoking or lost weight or started an exercise program, you can tell children your story about your struggle and success with changing that habit. Sometimes it's simple; other times it can be hard. But it is always possible to change a habit. Younger children love hearing stories about your struggles. Teenagers just roll their eyes. That's okay, they still hear you. Eye-rolling is just something they have to do.

REMEMBER THE BUMBLEBEES

Tell your child about aeronautical engineers who claim—beyond a shadow of a doubt—that the way bumblebees are designed makes it impossible for them to fly. But nobody told the bumblebees, so they fly anyway.

No matter how old children are, this story seems to resonate. When your children feel helpless or hopeless about their procrastinating ways, you can remind them of that bumblebee. It doesn't matter what other people say about them or what somebody might call them or what they have been calling themselves. They can change this habit of putting things off. Working with your child using these new concepts can help reduce communication difficulties within the family, and it's a terrific way for you to let your children know that you value them regardless of how they perform their chores and tasks.

Of course, communicating these "stop-putting-things-off" ideas with a child will take time and energy. But the payoff of having a responsible, happy child who can do what she sets out to do and who experiences success will certainly make it all worthwhile. It will also reduce stress on you and the family.

IS PROCRASTINATION INHERITED?

Parents are always asking, "Why does this child put everything off? Did she inherit a procrastinating gene from me because I'm that way?" or "Nobody in our family is a procrastinator. How did this happen to this child?"

Children often decide—sometimes before they can even speak or think logically—that it is beneficial to procrastinate. To understand how a child might make that decision, it is important to understand the oddities of children's logic, which most of the time does not even remotely resemble our logic. For example, a baby who crawls to the edge of a sofa and falls might be afraid of heights, but the baby could think, Last time I was on a sofa, I experienced pain. Therefore, sofas are bad.

Another example of children's logic: Kailey tells the story of when, on the day they installed their first extension phone, her brother Kevin called and her four-year-old son answered the phone. He saw Kailey walk past him, and when she went into the next room, she picked up the extension and said hello. Her son, in a very bewildered voice, asked her how she got to Uncle Kevin's house so fast.

And one more example of how bizarre a child's logic can

be: Jan said when her father passed away, she explained what a wake is to her five-year-old daughter, Sandy. Jan said that Grandpa's soul—the part of him that lived and loved and laughed—was up in heaven, and just his body would be in the coffin, and the family would go to see his body one last time and to say a prayer. Jan thought she had done a pretty good job explaining death to her daughter, but Sandy became hysterical about the wake and refused to go.

Later, Jan overheard Sandy describing a wake to some neighborhood children. Sandy said, "You know how when you draw a person, you draw the body and then put on the head and arms and legs. Well, just my Grandpa's body is in the coffin. I don't know what they did with his head and the rest of him."

Jan was stunned. After she reexplained and straightened everything out, she asked Sandy, "Didn't you think it was strange that we would go to see Grandpa's body without his head?" and Sandy told her, "Yes, but parents do strange things."

Children become procrastinators not in response to some traumatic moment but as a result of normal family experience processed through their odd logic. Some of what we do as parents inadvertently leads children to procrastinate. For example, it's important to raise children who don't expect instant gratification at all times. So we have to tell them on occasion:

"Not now. Later."

"I can't stop in the middle of bathing the baby to read you a story. You'll have to wait."

"I can't listen to you play the piano now, I'm late for work. Let's do that later."

Some children learn to be patient, to anticipate gratification. But others internalize another lesson altogether. They decide, I'm going to put things off, too.

Imagine that at age six, you picked up your toys while your brother just sat and watched TV. Dad comes home distracted about a business problem and says nothing about the toys. What conclusion might a six-year-old draw? Some might think nothing of it, but others might think, Hmmm, I might as well sit and watch TV and not pick up my toys anymore. Of course, this decision takes place in the subconscious mind, but this is where habits begin. Who knows why two children can be raised in the same house, and one turns out to be the world's greatest procrastinator, while the other never puts off anything?

ATTENTION!

Sometimes children will procrastinate simply to get attention. A high school teacher described an experiment from her classroom that helped everyone understand the power of "getting attention."

She was leading a discussion with a class of "gifted" sophomores; these were bright, well-behaved, perceptive teenagers. A student said that the opposite of love is hate, and the teacher responded that some say the opposite of love is indifference. As the class explored what this meant, the teacher said to them, "We know that most of us prefer 'positive attention' such as smiles, kind words, and friendliness. Now, let me ask you, if you could not receive positive attention, which would you rather have—negative attention such as frowns, hollering, and punishment, or no attention and just be ignored?"

Every single student in the class agreed they would prefer

to be ignored than to be yelled at or punished. One student said, "Nobody in her right mind would ever prefer negative attention!"

So the next day, when the students entered the classroom, the teacher was sitting at her desk, reading a book. After everyone sat down, she ignored them and continued reading. After waiting a while, the students started to call to her, "Hey, Mrs. G, what's up?" Their voices became louder, hollering. "Yo, hey, Mrs. G!"

At that, the teacher turned her back on them and continued reading. Gradually the students shouted louder and louder, and eventually these well-behaved, cream-of-the-crop teens started throwing pens, pencils, and wadded-up paper at the teacher's desk. Finally, someone threw a book that hit the wall with a loud crash.

The teacher jumped up, slammed her book shut, banged it down on her desk, then smiled at her startled students and said, "You just did exactly what I suspected you might do. You chose to try to make me angry—and maybe punish you—rather than allow me to continue ignoring you. Now let's discuss why you decided to behave the way you did, inviting negative attention instead of just letting me not give you any attention at all."

When children do their chores, we don't usually give them thanks or praise. Why should we? They're doing what they are supposed to be doing, right?

Some kids feel a sense of satisfaction in completing a chore without receiving any feedback. Others feel ignored, so they put off their chores. Then we parents rave and rant and fuss and punish, and although it doesn't seem to make sense, that child actually prefers negative attention to being ignored. A child may deliberately misbehave to get attention or may get his parents in a fury by doing nothing, by simply procrastinating.

Make every effort to catch children doing good or behaving well, and reinforce that behavior by giving that child attention and appreciation. Try to "head off at the pass" procrastination that's aimed at pushing your buttons.

Of course, as any parent knows, no advice works 100 percent of the time. Katrina, an intelligent mom who has read many parenting books, is very loving and encouraging toward her son. When her son was about two years old, Katrina was in her last month of pregnancy. She was sitting on a couch and told her son to put a toy back where he found it. She repeated, "Put it back," at least five times, and kept threatening, "Don't make me get up and make you put it back." He just stood there, looking at her and holding the toy.

"Finally I pushed myself off the couch," said Katrina, "and as I waddled toward him, he ran over and put the toy back where it belonged." So Katrina, being a nice, affirming mom, gave him a hug and a kiss and said, "There, isn't it better when you do what Mommy tells you to?"

But now, as Katrina reflects on the incident, she wonders what her son gleaned from her show of affection. "If he had put that toy away when I first told him to," she said, "I wouldn't have got off the couch, and he would not have received a hug or kiss. Maybe my son learned that it's better to do what Mommy says. But on the other hand, maybe he learned that by procrastinating and *not* doing it immediately, he received a nice hug and kiss."

We'll never know what went on in that little guy's mind that day, but Katrina marveled that a parent can do the same exact thing to three different children, and each will interpret the moment differently.

No parent would deliberately teach a child to procrastinate, but sometimes we'll do something that the child interprets as showing that it is to his benefit to put off a task.

HATE THOSE CONSEQUENCES

It breaks our hearts to see our children suffer a serious consequence for something they did (or didn't do). Samuel's daughter had put off a science project until the last minute, so he stayed up till midnight completing it. His daughter did not suffer any consequence at all. In fact, she may now think (subconsciously), Hmmm, when I put things off, somebody will come along and save me, and they might even do a better job than I could have anyway.

Samuel recognizes that attitude in one of his coworkers. The fellow leaves everything till the last minute, then goes running around the office, begging for someone to bail him out.

Another example of what most of us parents do, which seems innocent enough but can be a big lesson to our children about how good it is to procrastinate, is when children don't do their chores. Do you sometimes get so tired of reminding and pushing, and yes, even nagging, that you just do the chores yourself?

When the only consequence children pay for putting off chores is that we fuss a bit, but then do the work for them, they will become dependent and never develop the maturity and responsibility they need to become fully functioning people.

> Our children don't need our help to grow older, but they do need our guidance to mature.

Now—is this one more thing to become a nervous wreck over? "Oh, m'gosh, am I doing something that teaches my child to procrastinate?" No, not at all. Your child might develop the habit of procrastination for many reasons, most of them completely independent of anything you do or say. But there are strategies you can use to help your child turn around that putting-off habit.

Before you begin working through the tips and advice offered in this book, take a moment to understand some of the reasons your child may have resisted your previous efforts to curb his procrastination.

1. It may not seem like a problem to him if he never suffers any consequences from putting things off because someone (you, maybe?) keeps covering for him. The solution is to establish house rules that support doing tasks now: homework first, then TV; chores first, then get together with your friends; first a week of getting ready for school on time, then a trip to the mall.

2. Your child may be discouraged because she feels there is no hope for change. The solution: Explain that procrastination is just a habit; tell that bumblebee story. If you are working to blast away procrastination yourself, tell her about your journey and keep her posted on your progress.

3. Family communications may have broken down to the point of constant stress, anger, and resentment. In this case, procrastination is not the problem to be solved. It is a symptom of a bigger problem that needs to be addressed first, usually with the help of a professional.

4. Bad timing. If the child was just punished or yelled at, she is probably feeling embarrassed and angry. Most children will not be open to discussion or suggestions about their behavior at this point, so back off and give her time to cool down.

5. The child is oblivious. He may suffer consequences but forget about them once the episode had passed. Or he may not associate the consequences with the cause. The solution: Wait till the putting-off behavior occurs, and start pointing out reality to that child. Explain how life would be different if things were done on time.

Most parents feel that a child who procrastinates needs to learn self-discipline, and they often think of the word *discipline* only in terms of punishment. But *discipline* is defined in *Webster's New World Dictionary* as "training or teaching that develops self-control, character or orderliness and efficiency." Right now, by forming a team with your children, you'll be helping them learn life skills that will serve them forever in every capacity of their lives—and you might even find information that is helpful to *you* in your life.

TEAMWORK

This is your worksheet, to help you, not to make you anxious or guilty. You might decide to use none, part, or all of it.

Ideas to Discuss
——Procrastination is a habit; you can change.
——Tell the story of the aeronautical engineers who say bees can't fly.
——Negative consequences will be experienced if certain chores are not completed.

Ideas in Action

——Make up your mind to help your child stop procrastinating.

——Share stories about your experiences with procrastination.

——Develop house rules for "work first, play later" (either reinforce existing rules or introduce new house rules):

    ——Get input from spouse if new house rules are needed.

    ——Communicate with children about what new house rules will be.

——Keep your sense of humor.

2

The Power of Rewards

MANY CHILDREN (AND ADULTS) will look at a job they hate to do and think to themselves, Once I finish this job that I hate to do, there's just going to be another job that I hate to do, so why even bother doing the first one?

Here's a different way of looking at it. People who don't procrastinate ("anticrastinators") know that we all have jobs we hate to do. Nobody in the world lives a life free of these miserable jobs. But their secret is, when they finish that first miserable job, they don't move on to the next one. They pause and give themselves a reward.

Encourage your child by having rewards built into your house rules. The rules of the house should support doing tasks right away, while introducing your children to the "work/reward" idea. Declutter your room, then spend time on the computer. Take care of the pets, then go out with your friends.

A different kind of reward system should apply for those tasks that your child puts off that matter only to you, not the child. In other words, some kids do not care whether their laundry piles up or not, or if they take so long getting ready to leave the house with you that you're ready to go stark raving mad. This is where the majority of children are when you first start working at blasting away procrastination, and it almost always applies to young children. In this case, you need to supply a reward that really pleases or excites them.

This list might include something your youngster values as a reward, or it might trigger some other ideas. It's surprising how many rewards are the same for children of all ages, such as:

> going to a favorite place
> time with friends
> a special meal or treat
> computer time
> TV time
> a new CD or DVD
> new computer game or software
> money
> time out of the house
> new sports equipment
> something new for the child's room
> new clothes

Especially for Preschool or Primary Grades
> time with you or another favorite adult
> someone reading a favorite book to her
> a new toy
> a new book
> a trip to the playground, park, pool, or other favorite place
> a family outing
> time outdoors

going out to eat with you

any opportunity for you to pay attention to them

Especially for Middle Grades

(many of above plus)

work on a craft or project with you or another adult

membership in a youth group, sports team, or other
organization (example: not doing homework =
have to quit Scouts or team till grades improve)

a trip to the mall

overnight with friends

a trip to the pool

telephone time

Especially for Teens

(many of above plus)

chauffeur to activities

use of family car when she is old enough

a part-time job, including baby-sitting (for example,
poor grades = quit job = no money)

permission to go out

permission to stay out past curfew

this might surprise you, but some teens still cherish
time with you, going out to eat or to a favorite place

Team up with your child to make a list of rewards that he
or she loves. If your child can print or write, let her do it.
Even though the writing may not be as neat as yours, it helps
to reinforce that these rewards are her ideas, not yours.

Also, anytime you make a list together ("brainstorming"),
let the silly, negative, and nutty ideas get listed. It will help
both of you open up to new ideas; in addition, the value of

trying to get the child involved in the listing is that people usually accept their own ideas more than those of others.

Don't forget, the reward has to be convenient for you. It isn't reasonable for kids to expect you to take them to the park on a day when you are feeling sick. There needs to be respect for you here, too.

Some examples:

You might say to a young child, "Every night when you don't dawdle or argue about taking your bath, and if you're in bed by the time this kitchen timer dings, I'll read to you." (Or he can pick out which book you'll read; or offer him something else quiet and soothing). For the older ones, "You make it through the whole marking period without handing in any homework late, and I'll go with you to a movie, or shopping, or fishing, or a play, or a ballgame, or hiking, or to a Renaissance Faire, or out to a special breakfast, just you and me." You and your child can select the reward; make it something you both enjoy. This could be the beginning of a special tradition for the both of you.

> Don't forget that children overhear everything. Whether you're talking to the child or to other people, make sure that child hears you talking about the "do-it-now kid" and the new behavior of getting things done on time. That could be your child's favorite reward of all—hearing you brag about her.

At this point, many parents are thinking, No reward is ever going to work for my child. He doesn't have a hot button. *Nothing* will motivate that kid.

Allison thought the same about her eight-year-old daughter Emily. Alison said,

> I told Emily that there will be come changes around our house, and I'm serious about her doing her chores. She complains that she doesn't have time with me, but that's because I'm doing everything, including her chores.
>
> So I made up a chart of simple jobs, and she said, "I'm not doing those. I don't care if I don't go outside. I don't care if I don't watch TV. I don't care about anything. I'm not doing them."
>
> I just couldn't find a hot button. I guessed that she didn't have any. But one thing she'd been bugging me for was two songs she loved that she'd heard on the radio. I don't want her to have the whole CD (some of the other songs are objectionable) but these two songs were okay. I had them on my computer, and I was going to make her own CD for her with those songs she had really, really wanted. I told her that if she did her to-do list (she hated it when I called it a chore chart), then she could have her own CD at the end of the week with her two songs on it. With a very rebellious voice, she said, "I don't want those anymore. I don't want that as a prize." So I said, "Let's think about what you want," and she said she didn't want anything. Finally, later she came up with a prize of a small beanbag chair for her room, which we'd been planning on getting for her soon anyway.
>
> Her moods about this were up and down. First she'd be against everything I proposed, then she'd be cooperative. I was feeling discouraged as I printed up the to-do list, but then Emily took it from the printer before I came back to the computer, and I thought for sure she was going to rip it up into shreds. Instead she went and taped it up on the back of her bedroom door where she could see it. Then she hung an Aaron Carter poster right over it, so I thought she was going to forget about it by the next day.

But every day that week, she came home from school, lifted up the poster, checked the list, saw what she had to do, and did her chores. She puts her clothes in the hamper every day, then she can have dessert. She picks up her toys every day, and she gets thirty minutes outside. She vacuums three times a week, she gets to choose TV time or outside time. But halfway through the week, she asked if she could have the CD as her prize instead of the beanbag. I said that I thought she didn't want that CD, but she said that she changed her mind about the prize. That was fine with me.

Of course she *had* to push and ask for the whole CD, and I still said no.

In the end, I realized that I was right when I guessed that the CD would be the hot button, but Emily said no to be rebellious. I just had to be patient and wait for her to get over her crabbiness about having to do this work. Now she checks her to-do list with joy and enthusiasm, and she does a good job on her chores.

Even though you are supplying the reward (or prize, as Emily called it), let your children select what will get them going (with your approval, of course). When they feel that it is *their* choice, it will have a greater impact.

If neither of you can think of a reward that matters to the child, then the rule is, she has to earn what she usually takes for granted. For example:

- The preschool child: "If you cry and fuss about getting ready for church, then you'll have to skip playing any computer games today."
- The school-age child: "If you don't remember to write down your school assignments, then forget about watching TV tonight."
- The driving teen: "If you procrastinate about filling the

gas tank of my car when you use it, then don't count on using it for the next two weeks."

It's not realistic for a child to expect a giant reward for a little job. Children need to think about what is reasonable. If it would be terribly inconvenient for you to take your daughter to the mall after doing one chore, then that's not a reasonable reward, but maybe doing chores for a whole week *on time* and *without being reminded* might be worth your taking her to the mall for a few hours.

Ellen, the mother of three grade-school boys, helped them break their frantic-mornings-then-leaving-late-for-school habits by using bedtime as the reward. If they got ready in the morning without last-minute running around, they got to stay up a half hour later that night. But if Ellen had a hard time getting them out of bed in the morning, or if they just poked around or left everything till the last minute and left late for school, then she announced that they obviously needed more sleep and they had to get to bed earlier. In no time at all, they went one whole week without dawdling before school, so Ellen declared it a party, and they had pizza and rented a special movie for the evening. (Never mind that Ellen was going to order pizza anyway.)

When the dawdling had almost disappeared for several months, Ellen announced that a house without dawdlers deserved a family pass to the swimming pool, so they all went together to buy it. She also frequently commented on how much better their mornings were since they stopped dawdling and running around like nuts. She was surprised to find that after a while the boys started commenting on how pleasant their calm mornings were.

Even though you and your child may have decided on a

special reward to change a procrastination behavior, there's nothing to stop you or some other adult from "adding to the reward" when you see a sincere and persistent effort has been made. We are working on breaking a major destructive habit. If you can find a way to celebrate your child's success, go for it.

Paying Consequences

Negative consequences seem to be the opposite of rewards, but they are still part of a reward system. The house rules are often tied in with a loss of privilege or some sort of punishment.

"You know the rule, if your homework's not done [the consequence differs depending on the child's "hot button"], then no video games, or no computer, or no TV, or no time with friends." Many families have different consequences for each child, and the children soon figure out that *they* make the choices whether they are going to enjoy themselves or not, depending on whether they do what they are supposed to do.

You may find it hard to stick to the consequences or rewards that you've established for your child, but think about it.

- Would you rather be nagging them?
- Does nagging work for you?
- Does it lead to arguments or fights?
- Do you think you or your children really prefer fighting?
- Don't you find nagging, arguing, and fighting exhausting?

As adults, consequences are what keeps us in line most of the time.

If we speed, we get a ticket.

If we don't pay attention to the cake in the oven, it burns.

If we're late for work all the time, we receive a poor evaluation—maybe no raise, no promotion, or we could even be fired.

We learn to follow the rules in our lives, and so must our children. Sometimes parents complain about how difficult it is to enforce rules and consequences. Sean said, "I feel just terrible when she has to stay in and can't go out because her room isn't cleaned. I'm just a loving father, and I can't help it, I just give in to her."

It *is* hard to enforce the rules, especially if it means seeing your child sad or upset. But keep in mind that you're doing her no favor if you let her behavior slide until you're exasperated, and then nag and yell till everybody starts fighting and she's in tears.

It is more loving and supportive to enforce rules and consequences. That's the best way to help her stop procrastinating and learn to do what she's supposed to do. She'll be much happier in the long run.

THE RULE ENFORCEMENT TEAM

Think in terms of "partnering" with any adults who spend time with your child. Explain your house rules to discourage procrastination, and ask for their support and cooperation. These people might include:

- family or anyone who gives care to or in some way helps to raise this child
- teachers (they are not your enemies; they are your partners in teaching your child)
- an ex-spouse (even though you may be adversaries in other areas, make every effort to work as a team

in parenting your child, including this journey of helping your child become a do-it-now kid). Explain your efforts to your ex-spouse, describe your new house rules, ask for support in this area, and in exchange, offer to support any house rules in this area that your ex-spouse might initiate.

Ask about what rules they have that could help your child stop procrastinating and that you can support. Some of these people may not work with you in enforcing these rules, but it's worth a try to at least describe what you are doing, to explain the purpose of the rules and the importance of enforcing them, and to ask for their cooperation.

Are They "Real Rules"?

Children can learn to abide by rules as long as they believe they are real. But to find out whether they are real or not, they will push and test and see what they can get away with. Sean's daughter didn't believe that any of their rules were real because Dad always let her off the hook. That's what he thought a "loving father" did.

But once a child believes that rules are real, he will follow those rules even if they seem unreasonable to others. For example, fifteen-year-old Jason told me that when he goes paintballing, if you take your mask off once (to wipe paint off the viewer or just to look around) and a referee sees this, you are banned from the next two games. If the referee catches you with your mask off a second time, you're booted out of the field (or nest) *permanently.* You can never go back to that location; you must find a new place to paintball. This seems pretty harsh; these paintballers are usually teens, and this rule leaves no room for teen rebellion. But the participants know the rule is real, so if they choose to stay in the game, then they choose to follow the rules—whether they consider them to be reasonable or not.

If the parents keep sabotaging the consequences of breaking a house rule, then the children conclude that the rules aren't real; therefore, they don't have to obey any rules.

Most of the time, we as parents are the ones to provide consequences for our children. But if somebody else provides them, then we can offer support without having to enforce anything, and certainly we don't ever have to "fight" about it.

If he didn't practice his trumpet this week, then he will incur the music teacher's wrath. Maybe the rule is, "If you don't practice, you can't be in the band." We can sympathize and say, "Well, it sounds harsh, but that's the rule, so if it's important to you to be in the band, you know what you have to do."

Of course it's a different story if you feel the teacher is being abusive. But be careful. Some parents are driven to the brink of fury by their child procrastinating; then if he has to suffer a consequence in school, youth organization, band, or some other activity, the parent becomes defensive and overprotective. Some parents even join the child in offering a phony excuse about why he didn't do what he was supposed to do. Let the school and other organizations enforce their rules with your child. With your support, they might succeed in helping him conquer procrastination, without you having to get into a battle about it.

A Purple Monument to Procrastination

Adults and children both find it takes time to change a habit. Sometimes a change can happen overnight, but sometimes it may take months or more of reinforcing this new do-it-now behavior with rewards. For example, Frances used to wash her daughter's clothes, then put the clothes that don't go on hangers into a purple plastic basket and place it where ten-year-old Jessie sits to watch TV. Frances said, "That basket sits in the middle of the family room and sits and sits. Reminders are given *loudly* at least daily, yet Jessie ignores that purple basket, steps over it, and even trips on it. That basket is a purple monument to procrastination and an exhausting test of wills."

Obviously, Jessie doesn't care about the basket, but her mom does, and the rewards that Frances tried just didn't hit Jessie's hot button. Having clean clothes to wear wasn't enough of a reward for Jessie.

A friend suggested an alternative. "Stick the basket in her bedroom, close the door, and stop nagging," he said. "If this is the *only* thing she puts off, let her have her one little rebellion. If she puts off lots of other things, choose your battles and save your energy for the really important stuff."

I agree with him. This is not worth all that loud reminding (and probably arguments). Our energy and sanity are too precious for that kind of daily grind. But if you don't want to let it slide, a house rule would help—no going out with friends until your clothes are put away. And even then it's not worth a battle. When Jessie wants to go out or have a friend overnight, ask if the clothes are put away. If not, don't get into World War III; simply shrug and tell her, "You know what the answer is; you know the rules." She will eventually understand that she actually chooses the amount of freedom she receives, and that if you don't do what you're supposed to do, there is little freedom. Do what you're supposed to do, and you have lots more freedom.

> Choose your battles.

SELECTING REWARDS

After you have provided the reward for a while and you have your house rules in place about work first, then reward, the idea is to get your child to provide his own rewards.

Now let me warn you. It seems that no matter what age the

child is, when you talk to him about what rewards he can provide for himself, he will look at you in a sort of interested, unfocused way, and then the next words out of his mouth will be, "Like what?"

What to do? Brainstorm a list of rewards with him. All rewards won't need you to provide them; some might consist of gaining privileges such as spending time with friends or at the computer. So the child will determine how his time is spent depending on whether he does what he is supposed to do or not.

Some "self-provided rewards" apply only to mature children who have learned some self-discipline. After house rules have been in place for a while and have been enforced, the concept of work first, then reward becomes part of the child's routine.

For example, the five-year-old who knows that as soon as he's fed the dog he can select a DVD and put it in the player to watch is providing his own reward: choosing and watching the DVD. He doesn't have to wait till you are ready, he just turns it on himself.

An eleven-year-old who decides to get an early start on his piano practice Saturday morning because he wants to get outside in time for a ball game or the teen who says, "I don't let myself get engrossed in my sci-fi book till my homework's done," are both providing their own rewards. You don't have to give anything to them or take them anywhere.

Often, just the process of discussing possible rewards turns out to be a fun time together. Besides, you may learn something about your child. You may think you know what she considers to be a good reward, but there might be a surprise or two in there.

How and where do you have these discussions? You can

brainstorm while in the car, or waiting in line at the store, or waiting at the dentist's office. It doesn't have to be a formal "meeting" with both of you sitting staring at each other.

I'm an advocate of "car communication" for a lot of reasons:

1. When you're driving a gang of kids, either they forget you're there, or you become invisible (I'm not sure which), but they will discuss things in the car right in front of you that they ordinarily would never want you to know. Because of this, I always urge parents of teens to offer to drive them wherever they want to go. You'll be amazed at what you'll find out.

2. Some children just do not like conversations that involve eye contact, so sitting side by side in a car, or even talking while you drive and they are in the backseat, makes some children much more comfortable and willing to chat.

3. Some teens are more willing to talk to you when they know that the conversation will end soon (you are one block away from where they are going) than if they think the discussion will go on forever ("forever" to a teenager is about three minutes).

4. Most children are more willing to talk to their friends' parents than to their own (remember when you were a kid), so you can start a conversation when you have your child and a group of friends in the car. Your child's friends will sometimes answer your questions or start to discuss something, and your own child just might join in.

REALISTIC REWARDS

As she thinks of rewards, your child (and maybe you) need to be creative about it. What can she give herself? She'll be stumped at first. Maybe you can make some suggestions. For little ones, finish the chore, and then you can take the water-colors out to paint with. For big ones, finish the chore, then call your friend.

It has to be a meaningful reward. If it's something that is meaningful to you but meaningless to her, it won't motivate her and really becomes a useless strategy. And to say, "Well, finishing the job itself should be reward enough," is bogus—not only for children, but for adults also. If that were true, why in heaven's name would she have put it off in the first place?

The reward needs to be fairly immediate. The younger the child, the more immediate the reward must be: "As soon as you come home from school, put everything where it belongs; then you can spend time on the computer."

Help your child work out reasonable, realistic rewards—little rewards for little jobs; bigger rewards for big jobs. You're not going to take her on a trip to Disney World just because she cleaned her room.

If you have to be part of the reward, then you have to consider it to be reasonable. For some kids, money is a great incentive; for others, the amount of money they think they need to motivate themselves is not something a parent would consider to be reasonable.

Derek, who is four, knows that after breakfast he needs to get dressed, pick up his toys, and go get his shoes so his mom can help put them on; then he can watch his beloved cartoons. His mother has set up an allowance reward system based on what he gets done. The more toys picked up, the higher the denomination of coins he receives. He loves dinosaurs, so he is saving to pay half of the next dinosaur purchase. He loves this deal, enjoys watching his money grow in his piggy bank, and is learning about saving and managing money. On the days he is resistant, no TV, and little by little he loses privileges (chocolate milk, renting a movie, etc.), but he understands that he chooses the consequences by choosing whether he gets everything done first or not.

> Little rewards for little jobs; bigger rewards for big jobs.

Another mom gives her five-year-old one penny for each time he puts his clothes in the laundry *without being reminded*; he can then buy from Mom a sucker for three cents and an ice cream bar for five cents.

Most young children cherish time with you: "You help me set the table, and I'll play Chutes & Ladders with you."

Even older kids, including teens, are likely to appreciate or enjoy spending time with you if you are doing something they enjoy, and sometimes even if you're not.

Brainstorm with your kids about rewards; the most motivating ones will be those they choose for themselves. Watch their faces; when the right rewards are mentioned, their faces will light up, unless you're dealing with an especially sulky teen who would never be caught dead with a lit-up face.

Once they've brainstormed a list, post it where they can see it; use drawings or stickers if the child can't read.

Rewards do take some thought and creativity. Teachers, day-care workers, baby-sitters—anyone who spends time with your child—may have helpful suggestions. You could even team up with your child and ask her to help you brainstorm rewards for yourself; young children especially will suggest the kind of reward they'd want for themselves. If she goes through this process first with you, it could also make her own search for rewards easier and more comfortable.

Free time is a favorite reward for most adults, and for many children, too. Nora Bennett, a special education teacher, gives her students twenty-five minutes of free time at the end of the day as a reward: "Anybody with homework and class work completed and good behavior that day gets free time. It can be used for quiet activities indoors, or, in nice weather, it can be used for outdoor activity. And this is the best tool I have found.

"Everybody wants free time. Some children just like to be free to browse the classroom library; some play board games, use a computer, do their homework, have quiet conversations with their friends, do artwork, and on nice days, almost everybody wants to go outside, usually to play kickball. I have a classroom aide, so we can each supervise a different group."

TEACH YOUR CHILDREN WELL

A sharp, articulate woman wrote to me expressing regrets that no one coached her on overcoming procrastination when she was a child.

> I'm thirty-one years old. My biggest problem in school was putting off projects till the last minute, which led to rushing them and not feeling good about my work, and usually getting a poor mark. Ultimately, this led to poor self-esteem (it was not the only contributing factor) and overwhelming feelings of inadequacy, some of which are unfortunately still with me today.
>
> While I do not blame my parents, I wish they had pushed more when it came to homework. I never studied enough or spent adequate time on homework because nobody held me accountable. When I procrastinated, and ended up cramming for tests (99 per-

cent of the time, as it was all I ever knew), I got bad grades. I then got the "speech" about how "we know you're not stupid and you should be doing better and if you don't get a B on the next test you can't go to the . . . blah blah blah." It all seemed reasonable at the time, but in hindsight, nobody ever *showed* me how to pick away at a project bit by bit, so it would not seem overwhelming. I was never shown how to plan out studying time for each subject . . . you get the idea. Bottom line: parents should work *with* kids on this stuff. It will pave the way for success their entire lives—instead of just telling them to do it and lecturing when it doesn't happen.

Most likely your child does not enjoy being a procrastinator. It's up to you to help him or her find a different way of doing things.

TIPS TO SHARE WITH YOUR CHILD

Here's the **BUZZ** *about rewards.*

Be realistic & reasonable—a trip to Disney World would be nice, but you're not going to get that for cleaning your room.

Use your creativity—what can you give yourself? Complete a chore first and *then* go outside to play.

Zero in on a meaningful reward—so it means enough to you to really get you going.

Zoom in on a NOW reward—something you can enjoy soon after you finish your project or job.

TEAMWORK

Ideas to Discuss

——Work first, then reward.

——Positive consequences are experienced when children do not procrastinate (so *they* get to choose if "life is good" or not).

——Making lists can help.

——Does your child need anything to help him or her make a list?

THE NEXT STEP

Ideas in Action

——As a team, list ideas for rewards (you might be surprised at what your child loves as a reward).

or

——List rewards you will provide for your child doing certain tasks (money, transportation, a special meal).

——List rewards your child can provide for herself for doing certain tasks (privileges: time with friends, computer, or watching TV).

——Sometimes celebrate when you see an honest effort being made to change that procrastinating habit.

——Make sure you reinforce rules so your child knows the rules are real.

——Decide to drive kids and their friends more often.

——Try "car communication"; ask who procrastinates.

3

Solid Strategies for Overwhelmed Kids

You know how discouraged and exhausted you feel when you're overwhelmed with too much to do? Well, children feel the same way, but they are unlikely to know how to respond constructively to such stress.

They often can't see the light at the end of the tunnel when they have more than one subject of homework to do, or more than one chore to do. When they have their whole bedroom to clean up, they don't know where to start. Children can become overwhelmed easily. They don't realize that the trick is to break the job down into smaller chunks and pick one to do, rather than try to do them all at once. This may seem obvious to you, but it may be a new skill for your child to master.

At the end of each day, Mickey's two preschool sons were always overwhelmed at having to pick up all their toys. She remembered that when her oldest was in day care, the center had a rule: when you finish playing with one set of toys, you put everything away before taking out the next. All trucks would be put where they belong before pulling out building blocks, and so forth. So Mickey decided that since she was now a stay-at-home mom, she would incorporate this plan in her home.

Her five-year-old did fine with the new arrangement, but the three-year-old would not cooperate. So Mickey bought a tall wooden cabinet that resembled a nice-looking entertainment center, except that it locked. Almost all the toys fit in it, and the ones that didn't were packed away, to be brought out months later. Now both sons "trade in" whatever toys they have finished playing with before they can get another out of the cabinet. Mickey doesn't mind being interrupted during the day; it doesn't happen as often as you would think. Also, she's proud that the boys are learning the terrific skill of wrapping up one activity before starting the next—a skill that will serve them well in many other areas of their lives. And most important of all, the boys no longer are overwhelmed by the task of putting away their toys.

Encourage your child to formulate a plan before plunging into complex tasks. Ask him to select just one subject of homework for now, or do just that first chore. If the whole bedroom is to be cleaned, why not start by cleaning off the bed, then the floor? Or first pick up all the clothes, then take care of all the papers in the room.

Has your child heard those old sayings, "How do you eat an elephant? One bite at a time," or "How do you walk a mile? One step at a time?" Give him examples of when you were overwhelmed in your life and how you had to break those big projects down to doable jobs.

When Your Child Feels Overwhelmed

There's no age limit on feeling overwhelmed. Preschoolers are the right age for this topic; you might prevent a serious procrastination habit with the help you give them when they have too much to do. Older children are the right age because they can understand the concepts. Sarah describes this scene from her childhood: "I remember putting off my homework in elementary school until it was past my bedtime. . . . Then it was too late, and I'd lie in bed torturing myself for hours, worrying about the teacher being mad, and me looking bad in front of my classmates."

Children of all ages can experience anxiety about something they've been putting off, but young children seldom verbalize it. An older child might say, "I'm really nervous about that final exam," or "I have a stomachache about my book report," or "It gives me a headache to think about filling out those college applications." Of course older children, too, might have difficulty identifying and expressing feelings when they are overwhelmed.

Occasionally, if you know something big is coming and the child is avoiding it by putting it off, you can ask, "Do you ever feel butterflies or a knot in your stomach about memorizing your lines for the play?"

If your child admits it, you can explain that this kind of anxiety feeds on inaction. The less you study or prepare for what you fear, the worse your butterflies get. But the more time and energy you put into whatever you were putting off doing, the less anxious you'll feel. Older children really get this. Some younger ones do, and some don't. You can try it, or give them an example in your life. You can give guidance and suggestions to your child to help start an action plan:

- "Just read a chapter tonight for your book report; not the whole book, just one chapter."
- "To help memorize your lines for the play, read them into a tape recorder and play it back every chance you get, even when you're falling asleep."
- "For your college application, assemble everything you need into one notebook, so when you have time to fill it out, you'll have all the data and tools you need right at your fingertips."
- "Make a date to study with a friend for that final exam and don't let yourselves chat or goof off (well, at least not too much). Don't even have a snack till you've put in a solid hour of quizzing each other."

If your child has had trouble with feelings of anxiety, this will help him find instant relief. As soon as a person takes *some* action on what he or she has been putting off that is causing this severe stress, the anxiety tends to diminish.

THE LIST-MAKING TEAM (CAN EVEN INCLUDE LITTLE ONES)

Many adults find that when they are experiencing stress or anxiety because they are putting something off or feeling overwhelmed with too much to do, they write out a list of what needs to be done, and they feel more in control. Show your child how to make a list as a way to plan what she needs to do.

There are many ways to teach a child about making a list of things to do. You can help her write out a list when she is overwhelmed—a list that either breaks down a huge overwhelming project or itemizes all the many different jobs she has to do. Or you can talk to her about your list. Or leave your list posted on the refrigerator or some other conspicuous place so when she sees it, she'll be learning by example. Or make a big deal out of crossing items off your list. "Ta-dahhhhhh. I'm done!"

Olivia has a game plan for encouraging her three-year-old daughter to develop habits that will help her avoid procrastinating.

> My daily strategy includes organizing what I want to accomplish that day, then I share my list with my daughter when we enjoy our breakfast together. If I'm going to be busy with housework, or if we'll be running errands in the afternoon, she knows what we'll be doing most of the day. I think it helps her to see that we have a plan, and we usually do what we set out to do.
>
> The other thing that works well for us is keeping a project folder for Hannah (I actually keep one for me too). When she has an idea, and I know we can't do it right away, instead of just putting her and the project off, I suggest adding it to her project folder. That way we both know it's important enough to do at another time. It's great on a rainy day to have a folder full of things that she wants to do!

When you teach children about making lists, some take to it immediately, while others don't. Or your child might appear uninterested in making lists. Then a few weeks or months later, you might mention it again, and he looks up at you with wonder and says, "That's not a bad idea. Think I'll try it."

Also, don't be surprised if your child dismisses making lists several times when you suggest it. Then one day he announces that his coach is just brilliant because he gave him the best idea in the world—"Make a list of things to do. What a concept." If this has never happened to you, don't worry. It will.

SETTING PRIORITIES WHEN THERE'S JUST TOO MUCH TO DO

Young children have no sense of time, and most children have a poor sense of how long a project or task takes. They'll tell themselves, "I don't have time to do that, I'll wait until I have a whole Saturday free." Or another variation is that they will say, "I've been working on my homework for over an hour," yet every time you looked in on them, they were walking around in circles or tapping a pencil or staring at the ceiling or fiddling with a ruler, but they never touched a book. But they *think* they've really been working on their homework all evening.

It's time to talk to your child about priorities. No, that's not too big a word for a preschooler. You've been teaching them to break jobs down into small chunks; now the next step is helping them learn to select the most important chunk of work to do *first*.

TAMING THE TIME FACTOR

One of the best tips in the world, as well as a great way to help children start to get a sense of time about accomplishing tasks: get a kitchen timer and set it for a certain amount of time to work on that one priority—maybe one hour for kids twelve or older, thirty minutes for younger or short-attention-span children, and just five or ten minutes for preschoolers. You decide what's right for your child. Some children can focus for only five or ten minutes at first. It may not seem like a long time to you, but it's better than their doing nothing at all.

Some eight-year-olds can work a whole hour at a time on a project, whereas some adults can go only twenty minutes. It's not just age, it's attention span and energy level that you have to consider.

If your child has a hard time focusing, then start off with setting that timer for just ten minutes. However, while the timer is ticking, there are two simple rules to observe:

1. Do just that one priority. Don't start a bunch of other things.
2. No breaks. As a recovering procrastinator, I know that a really great procrastinator can take a thirty-minute job and have it last two months because she takes so many breaks.

TIPS TO SHARE WITH YOUR CHILD

Take the **STING** *out of feeling overwhelmed.*
Select one task you've been putting off.
Time yourself. Give the task one full hour.
Ignore everything else. Focus on doing just this one task.
No breaks allowed.
Give yourself a reward when the job is done.

By the way, there are timers out there in all kinds of crazy shapes. If your children respond to this, get them their own timers. Otherwise, every time someone is cooking in the kitchen, they'll have to chase all over the house looking for the kitchen timer. Let your children pick out their own timers.

So, what do you do when the timer dings and the child's time is up? It's time for a reward.

THE FORGETFUL CHILD

Children sometimes need a little extra support in the area of becoming organized. For example, if they are honestly forgetting to do things—walk the dog, make a phone call, study for a test, take a shower, or assemble their school gear—help them with making a list. Do they need something to write a list on? Do they need a place to put that list so it's not always misplaced? Do you need to go to an office supply store—with or without your children—to see what's available that might be helpful to them? Maybe a clipboard or maybe a special notebook or a way to carry their books or keep papers together. They need your help with this.

For prereaders, use a wall chart with pictures or stickers— a toothbrush, for example, to remind them to brush their teeth after meals.

Many adults need something to help them remember to do things. If your child is not doing homework, maybe the problem isn't the *doing* of the homework, it's the *remembering* to do the homework. You can help her figure out how to get organized.

Sit down with her and have her explain to you the step-by-step process of bringing home what she needs. Ask her questions so as she answers, she can decide, instead of you dictating to her. She is more likely to stick to decisions that she has made. For example, ask her:

- Does the teacher write assignments on the board? When?
- Does your child need a place to record assignments?
- What time during class can she do that?
- Where are her books at the end of the day? In her desk? Locker? Backpack?
- How can she decide what she needs to bring home?
- When and where will she be when she makes that decision?

Don't be afraid to work with your child. If we can help a child achieve a 10-, 20-, or 30-degree change, everyone wins. A complete 180-degree turnaround is just too much to expect right now. And don't forget, as you teach your children how to handle that overwhelmed feeling, that they are learning concepts and techniques many adults have never learned, and you are giving them a gift beyond anything money can buy. You are giving them hope.

TEAMWORK

Ideas to Discuss
——How to break the job into smaller chunks.
——That taking action on something makes the feelings of anxiety go away.
——Feeling overwhelmed.
——Do you make lists? If not, why not? Share your stories about making lists.

Ideas in Action

——Buy a timer. A cool one.

——Go to an office supply store and see if there is anything that will help your child to become organized.

——As a team, make a list of what your child needs to accomplish what she's been putting off (a chart to remind? a place to do homework? a scheduled time each night to do homework?).

——Purchase what your child needs.

4

"If I Don't Like It, I Shouldn't Have to Do It"

MOST PEOPLE—ADULTS AND CHILDREN ALIKE—know the misery of having to do something they hate to do. Often we put it off, dread it, feel guilty about it, but just can't push ourselves to do those miserable tasks.

The first step is to chat with your child about what he puts off. Pick out a task that he particularly hates and see if together you can figure out why it is so miserable. While you are driving your children somewhere is a fairly nonthreatening time to discuss this; you don't need a long sit-down, facing-each-other, eyeball-to-eyeball, formal conversation. Car communication is just fine.

Encourage your children to seek their own answers in these problem-solving quests. They are more likely to do it if the solution is something they thought of themselves. People do not argue with their own advice or ideas.

While walking to the park with six-year-old Elizabeth, Shannon asked her daughter why her clothes were constantly scattered all over her room. Shannon was pretty sure that it was because Elizabeth was always in a hurry and just didn't take the time to put things where they belonged.

But as she and Elizabeth chatted about it, Shannon was startled to hear that her little daughter was developing the same perfectionist tendencies that Shannon had. Elizabeth explained, "I can't make my clothes fit right on those stupid hangers. I hate them. And when I put clothes in my drawers, they get all smashed and bent, and I hate that. And if I try to stack stuff, it won't stay right."

For the first time, Shannon really heard her daughter's frustration plus her rock-solid resolution that if she couldn't put her clothes away "the right way," then she wouldn't do it at all.

When the words finally stopped pouring out of Elizabeth, Shannon asked her daughter what could be done about her messy room. After lots of banter and silly suggestions ("Give me your closet, Mommy"), Elizabeth said her girlfriend had wonderful hangers that kept her clothes from falling off; not stupid ones like Elizabeth had. Also, she was positive that she needed more drawers because her sweatshirts *had* to be separate from everything else. (There's that perfectionism, again.)

Last but not least, she was convinced that she needed a gadget inside her closet door where she could hang belts (she owned one), necklaces, and bracelets.

When they returned home, Shannon showed Elizabeth a small two-drawer nightstand that was stored in the basement. Elizabeth declared that it was perfect for her sweats, and later that week mother and daughter worked together painting it to match Elizabeth's room. She was thrilled with it, as well as the new, "right" (nonstupid) hangers her mom bought her. Then, as a reward for Elizabeth's great attitude (and because it cost only $5.95), Shannon bought that odd gadget for the closet door.

During the next several months, Shannon reports that her daughter made a tremendous improvement in keeping her clothes neatly put away, and has kept it up.

Paul and Monique did some problem-solving with their ten-year-old son, Tim, about doing his homework. The three of them sat down as a team, with Mom and Dad coaching Tim to write out a list of everything he needs to have handy when he does his homework. The first thing Tim wrote was, "a place." Paul said, "What do you mean, 'a place'? You have a perfectly good desk in your bedroom." Tim explained that it wasn't a good place. It was cold, and he couldn't stand working there. His parents made several suggestions for new locations for the desk. Tim rejected each one. He just did not want to do his homework at that desk.

Paul informed his son that the desk was his place to do homework—end of discussion. Then he stormed out of the room, but Monique hung in there with Tim and asked, "Where do you want to do homework?"

He told her, "At the dining room table."

His mom said there's no reason why he couldn't, but it seemed to her that he'd be distracted by the sound of the TV in the family room, and by his little sisters wandering in and out. Tim persisted, so his mom said yes. Then they continued with his list—he needed paper, pen, pencils, and a pencil sharpener. His father called from the other room, "Then you'll probably spend the whole evening wandering around gathering up all your stuff, right?"

Tim's solution was that he'd keep everything together in the top drawer of his desk, and every evening, right after dinner, he'd gather all his supplies, bring them to the table, and get started on his homework—without anyone reminding him. His mom added that if he kept his word for one month, he could have the overnight camp-out in the backyard that he'd been wanting. Tim did have to be reminded many times, but each time he settled down to his homework without arguing. Over the year, his grades have improved, he did have that camp-out, he still does his homework at the dining room table, and nobody understands why he won't do it at his desk. Not even Tim.

You might tell your children that in exchange for this "work" you are doing together (identifying hated tasks and figuring out what are the most miserable parts), you will help them the next few times that task has to be done, as an effort to seek solutions. This helps get momentum started.

Often, simply the process of discussing a problem reveals solutions. And although your children may not show it, they do notice that you are trying to help them find better ways to tackle their dreaded tasks. It's another way to show them that you care.

LET'S TALK ABOUT IT

During the morning drive to school, Sue mentioned to her fifteen-year-old daughter Jennifer how Sue was always putting off laundry because she just hated doing it. Sue said she realized, after having given it some thought, it wasn't the whole process of doing laundry that was miserable, it was just the folding and putting away of it. Sue asked Jennifer what her most miserable chore was and received the universal teen answer, "I don't know."

So Sue just kept talking. "I couldn't find my answer at first either, but when I really forced myself, I figured out what I hated and even figured out why."

At this point, Sue stopped talking, hoping Jennifer would be curious enough to ask why. After a long, very long pause, just as Sue was about to start talking again, she heard a small, sort of sulky, "So why?"

Sue responded, "Because it's *boring,* and there's not a thing you can do to speed it up. So now when I fold clothes, I'm going to catch up on family phone calls that I never have time to make. Next time you see me folding clothes, afterward you can ask me what's new in the family. *And* for my next birthday, I'm going to ask Dad and all of you to go in together and get me one of those phone headsets. You're going to have a high-tech mom.

"I even have a backup plan. I have a book on audiotape that I've been meaning to listen to for months. I might get into that while I'm folding, but I'm not going to spend time being bored folding clothes anymore."

At this point, they were almost at school, so Sue kiddingly said, "I'm not going to let you out of the car till you tell me your most hated, miserable, nasty, evil chore." Jennifer told her it was doing the dishes, and as she got out of the car, Sue called after her, "To be continued. We're going to analyze that, and once we know why you hate it, we might be able to make it less miserable." Jennifer called back, "I have the perfect solution, Mom—you do it."

There was lots more to discuss, but Sue was off and running. She had opened the subject with her daughter, and they even were joking about it.

It is easier to elicit discussions with younger children. When trying to talk to teens, the car seems to be the best place, especially when you are almost at your destination.

Other suggestions for trying to generate a discussion of what chores or tasks your children dread:

- Raise the subject when they are suffering a consequence of putting something off (such as being punished for not doing a task or receiving a failing grade for goofing off on homework and studying).
- After they have just loudly informed you that they hate, hate, hate doing something, ask them what part of it they hate most and why. (But wait till the heat of the moment has cooled down.)
- If your child and a friend or a group of friends are with you—sitting around the table, eating, or riding in a car—ask the most verbal child, "What's the thing you hate to do most?" If one child gets the conversation rolling, others (including yours) might join it.
- Take advantage of any of those wonderful, rare times that conversation is flowing. Watch for opportunities.

Getting to the Heart of the Problem

Let's say your daughter likes math, but continually procrastinates when it's time to do her math homework. Don't immediately assume that math is the problem. Watch, observe, ask a few pointed questions.

Sometimes you'll feel like a detective—looking for clues, trying to figure out a puzzle. But often, parents are working to solve problems without knowing what the *real* problem is.

Maybe it's not doing the homework that's the miserable part; perhaps the child simply needs a change of place or time. For example, if your children do their homework in front of the TV and the homework is handed in on time and done well, then there really isn't a problem. But if they are doing their homework in front of the TV and the homework is always late or done poorly, that situation is not working; they need a different, better spot to do homework.

Setting up a desk or a spot in their rooms isn't always the answer. Some children need quiet or privacy in order to work effectively, but others might feel isolated working in their rooms. Remember we're trying to find ways to make this task less miserable.

Some children do their best work where they can feel "connected" to the family; perhaps in the kitchen or dining room, where they can hear or see the rest of the gang. (This seemed to be the solution to Tim's problem earlier, remember?) Your child might be one who needs noise or music playing in order to concentrate. Ask him what HE thinks would help him get things done more effectively. Let the silly answers flow, laugh with him, and together try to figure out what will work and what won't.

A grade-school teacher tells the story of a family of five children where four of the siblings stay up late doing homework, but the fifth one chooses to get up at 5:00 A.M. to complete her work and study for tests. All five are allowed to follow their own time schedule as long as the work is done well (this family defines "well" as a grade of B or higher) and handed in on time.

Similarly, children have unique styles when it comes to doing chores. If they do the work in a different manner or time frame than you would, but if the final job is good quality, it might be worth letting them do it their way, eccentric though it may be.

Juanita deliberately leaves the kitchen whenever her nine-year-old son clears the table and loads the dishwasher because watching him makes her nervous. She said, "I can't explain it. It seems to me—the way he handles the dishes and glasses—that any moment he's going to break something. But he never does. He seems to make a game out of it, and control freak that I am, I become a basket case just watching him." Her son used to procrastinate about loading the dishwasher when she stood over him and criticized how he was doing it. Now that she leaves him to do the job on his own, he's more responsible, and she's less anxious, acknowledging that the final job is always completed as well as it would be by any adult, although he doesn't do it exactly the way she would.

Parents often notice that their children work much better when allowed to do their work in their own peculiar style. Perhaps it makes them feel powerful to do things differently from the way their parents wanted them to, or maybe it makes them feel unique, or they like to challenge themselves. Whatever the reason, if it works and it doesn't bother you, try to cut them some slack and be glad they are fulfilling their obligations.

TAKING THE MISERY OUT OF MISERABLE TASKS

Once you've helped your child determine what he most dislikes about a task he tends to put off, it's time for some creative problem-solving to see if there is any way to make that part of the task somehow less troublesome.

If he is having a hard time keeping his room clean, does he need something to help him? A larger wastebasket, his own laundry hamper, a special place to put stuffed animals, more drawer space for clothes or shelf space for books?

Most of us don't forget to do whatever we love, but it's easy to forget those hated tasks. Does he need some sort of reminder? A special notebook for jotting down homework assignments or a calendar to mark dates for activities or practice sessions?

One mom put a chart on each child's door listing everything that had to be accomplished in the morning so he could walk out the door prepared for school—get dressed, brush teeth, comb hair, eat breakfast, put dishes in dishwasher, pack lunches, gather books, lunch, and backpacks together, make beds, gather coats, gloves, and anything else he needs to wear when he leaves.

Some parents hang a second chart with tasks to be completed before going to bed. Use pictures, either drawn or cut from magazines, if your child does not yet read.

If your children have trouble finding shoes or books or their backpacks, try creating a special place by the door for each child to put her school things in when she comes home—perhaps a different-colored crate or plastic basket for each child. If children like their storage space, they are more likely to use it and put things away without constant reminders. *You* know where their things go, but do they? Yes, you told them once, but not everyone gets it the first time around.

If they dread practicing a musical instrument or practicing some other skill, perhaps a chart to mark down their time spent in practice will help. Or try audio- or videotaping a practice session once in a while so that seeing or hearing the progress they've made might generate some enthusiasm to offset the tedium of practicing.

Warning: As you attempt to establish good habits and routines, you'll notice that weekends sometimes seem to sabotage any sense of order, and everything seems to be thrown up for grabs. Your best bet is, every Monday, to simply reinforce practice sessions, study times, bedtime habits, and getting-ready rituals.

Make It a Game

Sometimes we can't take the misery out of the task itself, but we can try to turn the doing of the task into a game.

- Challenge your child: "I'll bet you can't do this in twenty minutes or by the time the timer dings."
- Teach him to challenge himself: "Can you do this faster than you did last time?"
- Teach him to estimate: "You've been putting this off for three hours. How long do you think it will take? I'll time you."
- Teach the children to blitz the house. "Let's all work to-

gether and get this place decluttered in one half hour. If we do, I'll take you to the pool and swim with you."

- Sing with them.

Some very little children will work hard while singing the "Barney Clean Up Song," and often they won't do a thing without the song. You might reach a point where you can't stand hearing the song one more time, but bear in mind that parents of teenagers would give anything for a song that would get their kids to do their chores.

Here are some creative examples of turning work into a game:

One Saturday afternoon, Sheila Glazov, professional speaker and author of *Princess Shayna's Invisible Visible Gift*, received a disturbing phone call from her 10-year-old grandson.

"Mimi, I need your help," he sobbed. "Matthew, what's the matter?" I anxiously inquired. "It's my Mom and Dad," he responded. "Are they ok?" I asked with great concern. "They're ok, but I need your help because they always listen to you and they are being very mean to me," he sobbed.

I was quite relieved to know that my family was not in harm's way and I figured anything Matthew was about to tell me could be handled. He proceeded to tell me that my daughter and son-in-law were making him weed the garden. He had put off weeding for several days after school and now that it was a beautiful Saturday afternoon he wanted to play with his friends.

I had to keep from laughing at the idea that his parents always listened to me. I suggested he count how many weeds he pulled and see how quickly he could finish. That way he could make a game out of the chore and make it into a fun project. He liked the idea. I told him to call me back once he had finished and let me know what his score was. About a half an hour later he called me back and said, "Mimi, I did it! I finished picking 150 weeds in 30 minutes." "Matthew, you're a real champion and I am so very proud of you," I told him. We both laughed and I told him the next time his grandfather and I came to visit we would have a weed picking contest!

Brainstorm with your children ways to make their tasks more fun. Or introduce them to negotiating and suggest that they try to swap their hated chore for something less miserable. If they can get a sibling to go along with them, they'll be doing the chore of their choice.

Diane, now a grandmother, devised a game when her children were small. It got her children not only to do their chores but to do them in a timely manner.

"My kids used to enjoy 'helping Mommy' when they were little," says Diane,

But by the time my two were in the eight-to-ten-year-old range, I found that things had changed. They were less cooperative, and I was becoming a nagger. "Brynn, you haven't made your bed yet," or "Tom, you haven't cleaned your bedroom, I see." During summer break I decided to stop nagging and began writing out a list for each of them every morning.

The lists worked fine, and the chores would get done . . . eventually, but what's the point of making one's bed at seven in the evening? The list didn't have a time limit, and I found myself again in the role of ogre, "Haven't you taken the garbage out *yet*?"

One further refinement of my system did the trick. By 6:00 A.M. I would have two lists posted on the refrigerator, List A and List B. Each list would have similar chores, such as "Make your bed and straighten your bedroom," but also a few dissimilar ones. For example, only List A would have "Fold towels and put away," and only List B would have "Vacuum family room carpet." Some chores appealed to Tom, others were less objectionable to Brynn. The effect was that they each tried to be the first to the refrigerator in the morning to claim the "best" list. They then had to actually begin within a reasonable amount of time to do their list.

It worked for me. I got some help, I didn't need to be the "slave driver," and Tom and Brynn felt a bit of control of their day as well as developing a work ethic."

Maybe we can't change or delete the misery of a chore, but sometimes doing it can be turned into something silly or fun.

A Little Help from a Friend

As you search for ways to help your children make their dreaded chores less miserable, think of what a delight it is when someone has joined in and helped you with a job—whether at work or at home. You can offer that gift to your children.

This is not the same as giving in to children who have cried or fussed or thrown tantrums until somebody offers to help them or bail them out. That's called manipulation.

Let them know you'll help them, but on your terms. Tell them, "Look, if I see you make an honest effort to do a good job *with a good attitude* today, then there's a very great chance that after you've been working ten minutes or so, I just might come in and help you finish." They need to hear over and over that the good attitude will get rewarded, but the bad attitude will not.

No matter what the age, you can work with them cleaning their rooms, closets, or drawers. In the process, you are teaching them how to do the task. Often parents presume that children know how to do something because you showed them how to do it once or twice. But the child may not have grasped all your instructions and might be muddling along without a clue as to how to do the job.

Maybe they start making the bed, then stop to hang up clothes, but before they finish that, they start tossing papers into the wastebasket until it's overflowing and has to be emptied. An hour can pass, and they're not much closer to being finished. If you don't have a workable plan for completing a chore, these half-finished tasks can make any job a drudgery. You may need to give explicit advice on how to do a chore, even if the details seem painfully obvious to you. One example:

Steps to Cleaning a Bedroom
1. Clothes: hang up or put away clean ones; put all dirty clothes in a laundry bag, basket, or hamper.
2. Papers or anything else that should be thrown away: put in wastebasket or trash bag.
3. Books, papers to keep, toys, other stuff to keep: put away one category at a time (put papers in a notebook, books on shelf, everything else where it goes).
4. Anything else left on floor, bed, or other surfaces (dresser top, desktop) that doesn't belong there: put away where it belongs. If it belongs in another room, deliver it there now.

Then, if your child is old enough and capable, he should continue:

5. Make the bed.
6. Empty wastebasket.

7. Dust.
8. Sweep or vacuum floor.

Sometimes children procrastinate simply because they really don't know how to do what they are supposed to be doing. They never really learned how to make a bed, set the table, load a dishwasher, do yard work—whatever the chore. So even though they may have been doing this chore for a long time, working with them will help you observe whether they need some tips or instruction. Or maybe they know *how* to do it, but you can show them ways to do it faster, better, or easier. Set the timer to see if you and the child as a team can beat a previous time spent on this chore.

Warning: Many parents are dismayed when after working with their children and watching them master chores and start to do a terrific job, these same children grow into teenagers, and all the good work seems to have been wasted. Teens are notoriously preoccupied, forgetful, and awkward, and often it seems that their brains fly out of their heads. You'd be smart to occasionally spend some time again working with your teen child on a few chores. When it comes to teenagers doing chores, there seems to be frequent . . . um . . . regression.

Besides being a form of training, working with a child can be a fun way to chat and communicate. It's an opportunity to catch up on what is happening in her world—and your child is receiving your undivided attention.

Spending ten minutes "playing pickup" to help a three-year-old clean her room, teaching her how to put books and toys in the right spot and how to hang up some clothes, put the other clean clothes away, and put dirty clothes in the hamper, is much more effective and enjoyable than spending all morning yelling at and nagging her.

Some families make it a tradition that on school holidays or during vacation, a parent or relative spends an afternoon with a child sorting through closets and dresser drawers. Besides being a chance to catch up with each other, it's helpful to any of us to have someone encouraging us to "get rid of our junk."

Warning: Some children are especially attached to their mementos. There might be some ideas in chapter 8, on clutter busting, that would help here. Also, it's not unusual that a child who used to be pretty easygoing about tossing out stuff will suddenly hit the teen years and not want to part with anything (especially during the last year of school). Unless there is an unusual circumstance, let it be. Give it time and "revisit" that project in another year or so. (For more ideas about helping children organize and de-clutter their rooms, see chapter 8.)

Another option is to make a deal to help a child with a chore *if* that child will then help you with whatever project you are working on.

Other ideas for making chores less miserable are to let two children work on a job together (some can work together, others never can) or play their music while working or have a friend over to keep them company while they work, if the friend's presence isn't too much of a distraction.

Maybe none of these solutions will work for you, but you get the idea. Use some creative problem-solving to help make a little less miserable those jobs that your children always put off because they just hate to do them.

When children hate doing something because it's a miserable job, they have the uncanny ability to spread that misery around to everyone within earshot. Many parents want to give in and do the job themselves rather than endure the whining and complaining. Kerry, the mother of two young daughters, said, "I often was tempted to complete the task myself; it would seem quicker and less mentally exhausting. But when I'd force myself to wait it out, often after just a few times of listening to their pathetic complaints, they'd improve and get going."

If we finish our children's work, not only will they learn that when they whine and complain, we will bail them out; they will also receive a message that they are incapable and incompetent. In addition, some kids really take great joy in reducing their parents to yelling and screaming when they put things off. However, when you encourage children to accomplish their tasks, with or without your occasional assistance, you foster feelings of self-reliance and pride.

FEELINGS—NOTHING MORE THAN FEELINGS

Sometimes, when you start to talk with your children about the tasks that they put off because they hate to do them, they focus on how miserable they will feel. "It's hard," or "It's boring," they whine, and often you agree that, yes, it *is* a hard or boring project. Emptying the garbage will be a smelly, unpleasant task, regardless of what you do to try to make it less dreadful.

Your child needs to focus on how she will feel when the job or project is *completed*, not on how miserable she will feel while *doing* it.

It's important to point out to children that everyone has some kind of messy or icky or miserable work to perform; that's just a fact of life. When kids feel put upon or weighed down by life's crummy tasks, they tend to believe that others are living happily ever after, and they alone have been struck down by some evil stroke of fate. They spend hours, days, and weeks regretting that they were born to a life of having to do miserable chores. They are convinced that other people have only wonderful, joyous, exhilarating tasks to do.

Tell your child that there is an upside and a downside to every single thing in life—every occupation, every person, has to do some miserable, crummy, hated jobs. Share with them some of the downside to things that sound wonderful —holiday celebrations, wonderful-sounding careers, owning a home, traveling (Let's hear it for the joys of lost luggage!).

The second half of this "attitude adjustment" is: Explain that the sooner they accept the fact that their lives will always include miserable tasks and chores, the less frustrated they will be, so they may as well stop complaining about it, because that only bums everyone out.

DO THE WORST FIRST

You've probably heard it all your life. Do the worst job first. Get it over with. My grandmother used to say, "Do it and be done with it." But have our children heard this . . . ever? In this era of instant gratification and taking the easy way out, our children possibly have never heard—have never been taught—that premise.

It's up to you to make sure your child knows and grasps this principle. You know what it is to push a miserable job aside and have it hang over you all day long, with the dread of doing it draining your energy. Help your child understand the relief and freedom that comes with getting that terrible task out of the way first, then being free of it for the rest of the day.

Teach him to rejoice and celebrate when he has finally completed something that he has been putting off (or that he used to put off but doesn't anymore). Remember how terrific YOU felt when you finally completed something you'd been putting off?

TIPS TO SHARE WITH YOUR CHILD

Let **HONEY** *sweeten those crummy jobs you hate to do.*

How can you make it less miserable?

Only focus on how you'll feel afterward, not how you'll feel doing the job.

Name a great reward ahead of time.

Expect to do crummy jobs in your life. Everyone has to do them sometimes.

Yell out, "I did the crummy job first. Now I'm free!"

TEAMWORK

Ideas to Discuss

——What is this child's most hated task? What is the most miserable part of that task?

——Does the child need tools or something that would help make the job less miserable?

——Focus on how you'll feel when the job is complete, not how you'll feel while doing it.

———Everybody has to do crummy jobs in their lives.

———Do the worst job first.

THE NEXT STEP

Ideas in Action

———Pay attention to what might be the real problem.

———As a team, list ways to make the job less miserable.

———Help your child break the hated task into doable steps; list the steps.

———Purchase a wastebasket, clothes hamper, etc., if children need these things to keep their rooms organized.

5

Extinguish Excuses

CHILDREN OFTEN THINK THAT many aspects of their lives are out of their control, especially their procrastination. When they can't get themselves to do something, they feel that they are so backed against the wall that their only recourse is an excuse. It's the only behavior that explains to the rest of the world why they are acting the way they are. Very often, they themselves don't have a clue why they are procrastinating. So they make up an excuse in order for their actions to make sense.

"My homework? What? I did it in study hall. . . . Uhh, I think I handed it in, let me check now. . . . Where did it go, where did it go? You know, I didn't hand it in yet—the teacher was not in, she was out sick. . . . Yeah, that's it. Now I remember. She was sick!"

Excuses are particularly frustrating for parents, teachers, and other caregivers, because it's so hard to respond constructively to the tales kids tell to cover up their procrastination. Sometimes the child may be lying, but keep in mind that many children do not have a clear sense of what is real and what isn't, so when they give phony excuses for why they still haven't accomplished an assignment, they often truly believe them. (The phenomenon applies to some adults, too.) Many children just don't understand cause and effect. They don't realize that when they put something off (they haven't fed the fish in three weeks), it causes something to happen (the fish are floating belly-up). All they know is that they are in trouble and it has something to do with dead fish.

Procrastination carries with it a great deal of shame. People of all ages often find it embarrassing to admit that their own putting-off habit is the real cause of their troubles. They would rather put the blame on someone else or, if that's not possible, come up with a story to explain why they could not do what they were supposed to.

When you approach children about excuses, don't even touch on reality, truth, untruth, or any of that. Instead, guide them in understanding the difference between phony excuses versus real reasons. When people suspect that others won't agree or approve of their reasoning, it's common for them to offer the most logical reason that they think will satisfy the other person, instead of giving the real reason.

Have you ever been with a fast-talking salesperson, when you don't want to buy the product because you've heard that service is terrible? You *know* that if you tell that to the salesperson, you will receive a strong argument. So rather than argue, you offer an excuse: "I have one already," or "I can't afford it."

Start with helping your children recognize phony excuses. Point them out whenever you encounter them—on TV, from others, even from yourself. Point out examples, too, of people owning up to their procrastinating or "blowing an assignment." As children begin to grasp the difference between accepting responsibility for one's behavior and giving lame excuses, also help them search for solutions, just in case there is something real to their excuses.

- "I didn't have time." Teach them about priorities and doing either the most important things or the most unpleasant jobs first. But is it possible that they are overscheduled and really don't have time to get everything done that they are supposed to? Help them with their schedules and have them explain to you why they don't have time.
- "I forgot." Help them devise a system to remember— a list, a calendar, a PDA (personal digital assistant), or a chart. If they don't want to work on a system, then they are saying that their memory will do. Let them try. If they do start to remember to do what they are supposed to do, fine. No problem. But if they keep forgetting, then insist on a system.
- "I don't know how." Teach them or arrange for after-school tutorial. Chances are it will become evident fairly quickly whether the child really doesn't know how to do his work or is just making an excuse.
- "I'm too little." If you're big enough to make that mess, you're big enough to clean it up. A child as young as two or three years old can learn to work with a rag and clean up spilled milk, even though you'll still need to help out. Including the child with the task builds positive self-esteem.
- "I didn't know I was supposed to do it." No matter how old they are, they might need a chart or some kind of reminder posted someplace in the house.
- "The computer ate my homework." If you've ever worked on a computer, you know the agony of losing

all your work (and how stupid you feel). You have to do your work all over again. But you learn your lesson: you back up often, and, in case you run into problems, you don't wait till the last minute to print your work. Your children will learn the same way you did, as long as you don't rescue them and re-do their work for them. If you do that, they will never learn, and homework will suddenly become *your* job.

Whatever the excuse is, look to see if you can help them find a solution for it.

THE "YEAH-BUT-RABBIT . . ."

The "Yeah-But Rabbit" is a clever variation on an excuse. It appears when we remind our children that it's time to get ready for school, and we hear, "Yeah, but first I've got to finish reading this book." Or we say, "That poor dog has been waiting a half hour for you to take him out!" and we hear, "Yeah, but I'm too busy doing school stuff."

Kids may put off doing something because they want to do something else, and the excuse is aimed at convincing you that what they want to do is more important. Instead of, "I can't do that because . . . ," it's, "Yeah, but this is so very, very, very much more important, don'cha know?"

They will turn it into a power play, and they will insist on putting great importance on the looniest things—picking fuzzie-wuzzies off a sweater, watching a cartoon that they've seen a hundred times, searching their room for a missing teddy bear that nobody has seen in years. They simply *have* to finish this important task, even if they've never done it before in their lives.

A Mindless Mind Game

Procrastination is a mind game. Often, excuses (including the Yeah-But Rabbit) are power plays or rebellion on the child's part: "I'm going to show you who's boss, who's in control around here."

Peggy complains that while her nine-year-old son is playing a video game, "I'll tell him I need a chore done, or even to come to supper. He'll want to finish or save his game, so he'll tell me 'In a minute, I'm almost to where I can save.' That's fine, so I'll come back in ten minutes, and he'll say, 'Not now, I'm in a battle!' Then, given an ultimatum, he'll put me off again and sometimes even change games, thinking that I'm not paying attention to him. When I get angry, *he* gets angry, stomps around, growls, flings his game away, and then gets grounded."

It's time for Peggy to find her son's "hot button" (see chapter 2), which might be a privilege he'd lose that would be meaningful to him. Grounding him doesn't seem to bother him, because he continues the same behavior. It's not important to him, but apparently his video game is. So the next time he puts her off, Peggy should forget about grounding him and calmly take the game away. Or better yet, if he dares to fling it again, she can simply pick it up and tuck it away someplace for whatever length of time she determines.

Peggy's house needs a new rule—something like, If you use a game as a reason to procrastinate about something that you are supposed to do, then no games for the next two days.

Now Peggy discusses her other son. "My eleven-year-old son will have homework. This has happened more than once. I'll ask him if he has any, and he'll say no. From past experience, I'll check his backpack, then ask him what the books are for. He says, 'Oh, I forgot! It's only a little bit, can I do it after supper?' Since it's only a little, I think it's okay. Then, when it's time for him to start, suddenly he tells me he has a project, or a book report, or three biographies due *tomorrow*! Then he fidgets and whines for an hour, wants a snack, a drink, even cries, telling me that it's just too much to do. And when I finally force him to begin, he's through in fifteen minutes! Two hours of misery for fifteen minutes of work."

This house may need a new rule for a "designated study time" when this son cannot do anything but his schoolwork. (More on this later in the chapter.) Then, if he continues to procrastinate by fidgeting and whining, that study time might be lengthened.

Before this new rule goes into effect, he may need some help getting organized. Peggy could encourage him to make a list of all he needs to do and gather together to get started, and a second list of the steps he has to take to do his homework. And maybe setting a time limit for that "preparation time" would help: "Okay, set the timer for five minutes to get started. When it dings, it's time to settle down to work on your studies." This type of structure helps out-of-focus children to focus on one thing at a time. First gather what you need; now start your work. Follow your list of what you have to do.

Here are examples of two lists made up by another eleven-year-old boy who obviously enjoyed needling his mother:

List #1: Prepare
  1. Get books and paper.
  2. Get pens and pencils.
  3. Make sure pencils are sharp.

4. Call Terrell to double-check homework assignment.
5. Remember to talk fast, since I only have five minutes to get ready.
6. Get a glass of orange juice.
7. Get timer so I know when my study time is up.
8. Go to bathroom because my cruel mother won't let me leave my desk once I get started.
9. Check my jacket pockets and backpack to see if I have any more notes written about what I should do for my homework.

List #2: Do homework
1. Clear off desk.
2. Read all my assignments.
3. Pick out one subject to do.
4. Reread that assignment.
5. Take out book, paper, or notebook that I need.
6. Start at beginning and go to the end of that assignment.
7. Take a break. My cruel mother allows me to stand up and stretch and get another glass of orange juice after I finish the first assignment.
8. Do it again with next subject.
9. Do it again and again and again and again and again.
10. Tell cruel mother when I am finished.
11. Collapse from exhaustion.

The young fellow who created these two lists kept both posted above his desk and referred to them frequently. It was a great help in improving his attention span and keeping him focused. It also cut down on the fights, whining, and, most of all, procrastination.

MOVING THEM ALONG

When a child is in this game mode of putting off parents, and a parent decides to fight it, the results most often are lose/lose, resulting in the War of the Worlds. You might end up yelling or being so frustrated that you lose your temper, while the child ends up in some sort of fury. You'd rather avoid an inevitable fight, so when it's possible and appropriate, give your child a way to back out gracefully: "Yes, yes, I realize this is only the eighteenth time you've seen this; I'll give you five more minutes, then you're expected to grace us with an appearance at the dinner table."

Or sometimes you can kid around: "I understand that you have to finish this enormously important task of rearranging

your shoelaces, because we all know what catastrophes can happen when shoelaces are uneven, so when can we set an appointment for you to take out the garbage?" However you approach it, pin him down to a definite time: "So tell me when you'll start cleaning the kitchen? Five minutes? Ten? Just give me a time."

For a little kid who isn't great at telling time, set the timer. "Okay, when this dings, you're going to go outside and put away all the toys in the yard, right?" Bigger children can watch the clock or tell time by the program they are watching: "Okay, when this show's over, you're going to write that thank-you note to your godmother, right?"

This mind game gives them a sense of power. If your child uses phony excuses all the time, then realize that procrastination is not the problem here. Putting things off is just a symptom of a defiance, a rebellion, or some difficulty in your relationship with that child or some problem she hasn't been able to work out, and neither this book nor fighting with her is going to solve it. You probably need some sessions with a professional to give you guidance in parenting this child during this period of her life.

However, sometimes just exaggerating the situation and asking her to set a time can move things along: "I understand how terribly, terribly important it is to this household that you arrange every single one of your eight million dinosaurs in a nice, single, perfect file across your dresser, but those poor little cats have to be fed today. Please tell me when you will prepare a sumptuous dinner for the kitties?" This gives you a chance to back out and try another approach to uncover the problem. Something must be bothering this child if she has to try to bait you to start a royal battle like this.

One other approach that some parents have luck with is distracting children who are ready to blow up. When children decide to dig their heels in and start a fight, some parents move the whole conversation to something else. One dad starts to "do the tango" with his two-year-old daughter, then comes back to the subject of doing what needs to be done at a later, more calm time. Some parents may think this kind of diversion is coddling a child and letting her have her way; but keep in mind that your goal is to help children stop procrastinating. When procrastination situations arise, don't automatically take the bait from a child who would rather fight with you than do what he's been putting off. Pause a moment to ask yourself whether this particular situation is something you want to fight over, possibly hurting your relationship with your child. If distracting a child heads off a blowup or fight, what harm has been done? As mentioned earlier, choose your battles.

A "Dedicated Study Time"

Sometimes, these fights and furies can be avoided by what some parents call "dedicated study time." This is a nonnegotiable chunk of time set aside each day when the child does nothing but homework

Brianne's son Todd, who has been diagnosed with a mild case of AD/HD (attention deficit hyperactivity disorder), has terrible trouble focusing and getting things done, and he's disorganized. She describes their homework solution:

"We set up a specific time frame in which Todd must complete his homework (4:00–4:45 P.M.). He must use the entire time to do his homework rather than rushing through and getting finished in twenty minutes. If he finishes before 4:45, he can spend the remaining time reading a book or reviewing his work."

At first Todd resisted the set time, but Brianne would not give in. *Nothing* was allowed until this forty-five-minute time period dedicated to homework was completed—no TV, no computer, no friends, no time outdoors, not even dinner. The family sat down to eat, and Todd could not join them until he put in his forty-five minutes doing homework.

In the beginning, it took a great deal of policing and patience on the part of the parents, but before the end of the first week, Todd knew they meant business; he knew this was a "real rule," so he eventually accepted this new family procedure. His favorite reward was that when his grades came up, he would get paroled (as he called it) once in a while, and would be allowed to skip the mandatory forty-five-minute study period.

C. J. Jonasen, a high school Spanish teacher, will sometimes give her students dedicated study time to work under supervision on their big projects; she also helps them as a group to set attainable goals. "Occasionally some kids will just 'take that period off' and swear to me they can do a better job on their home computers," she says. Like anything in life, some of her students benefited from having dedicated time set before them, and others were impervious to this help.

REFOCUSING

You know those days when you feel you must be going around in circles because you can't focus on anything, and the whole afternoon, maybe even the whole day, is gone, and you have accomplished nothing and wonder where the time went? Well, your children occasionally may do the same thing.

Instead of focusing on what they are supposed to do, children sometimes drift, stare out the window, spin the wheels on a toy car, wander around the room, or doodle. Then they look you in the eye and whine or sob, complaining, "It's toooooooo hard, and it takes toooooooooo long. I've been working on this all day."

Yuki's daughter would stand in the middle of the family room, stretch out her arms, and spin around in circles—nothing else, just spin. Yet she would come and collapse next to Yuki in an exhausted heap, and wail at the top of her lungs that she had been dusting the family room all morning long and still wasn't finished, and she needed Mom to help her. So one day Yuki went with her into the family room, stood in the middle, said, "Okay, sweetie, I'll work right along with you," and started to spin. Her daughter failed to see the humor in it that morning, but Yuki's three best friends supported her, and one of them decreed that sometimes the only thing you can do to keep your sanity is to spin in circles.

Another said, "It probably was every bit as effective as nagging her or yelling at her or threatening to punish her." As parents need to remind themselves every single day, above all, keep your sense of humor.

When your children find it hard to focus and instead fiddle or dawdle or goof off, bring out the timer again. Coach them to set it for ten minutes or thirty minutes (or whatever is best for your child) and do just one task. No breaks. Don't do anything else. Then they are through. The amazing thing is, once the chore is complete, they usually settle down and stop fiddling or whatever it was they did when they were "out of focus."

Appearing Daily at a Bathroom Near You

~~~~~

Sometimes, kids' reasons for not doing something are real, or seem real to them. For example, they are in a hurry getting ready for school in the morning and try to convince you that they really don't have time to clean up any mess in the bathroom. They leave water splattered all over the place, towels are dumped on the floor, toothpaste is smeared on the counter. They insist (and believe) that they don't have time to clean a whole bathroom.

Josh grew tired of the daily mess, so one day he calmly and patiently led his teenager, Thad, into the bathroom, and handed him a stopwatch. He had Thad time him as he demonstrated how long it takes to hang up a towel, wipe off a counter, and put away toothpaste. Then Josh had Thad enter each time into a notebook, add up all the seconds, and tell Josh the total time that cleanup took. Josh didn't yell or preach or punish. He just calmly presented his bathroom demonstration day after day until Thad started cleaning up after himself. Josh believes Thad decided that doing it himself was easier than enduring his dad's crazy, time-consuming demonstrations.

"I could hardly keep a straight face while I was doing it," Josh admitted, "but I acted very sincere in my demonstrations. We might as well have fun while we're teaching our kids. If you can't motivate them, bore the daylights out of them. It worked for me."

Back-Timing Is Forward-Thinking

Have you ever seen a look of amazed surprise on your child's face when it's time to leave for your nephew's wedding or a similarly important occasion, the whole family is dressed, looking gorgeous, waiting in the car, and she comes swinging around into the driveway, wearing muddy jeans? She looks at you with an innocent, unbelieving expression and says, "Oh, is it already time to go?

Some kids are con artists, but many just have no sense of time. They could grow up to be those adults who leave at 8:45 to start work at 9:00, but live one hour from work. This type of person arrives late *every day* for work, and is actually surprised *every day* that she is late.

People who never allow enough time to arrive when they are supposed to, as well as people who leave everything until the deadline is upon them, can profit from learning how to back-time.

The objective of back-timing is to work backward by setting fake or target deadlines. Children tend not to pay any attention to a deadline until it is smack in their face. Then they finally get started, but of course it's way too late.

Start with helping them get a sense of time. They might benefit from a bulletin board in their room where they can post a huge sign giving due dates or times, or a calendar. This is helpful only if they use it, though; sometimes parents think that just because a child has a calendar in her room, she will look at it every day. Therefore, that child should know what today's date is. But her idea of the purpose for that calendar may be the "great pictures."

Some children have had calendars hanging on their walls for years, yet not once have ever looked at it or even cared what the date was. It doesn't help to mark a due date on a calendar that is not looked at. You have to discuss the due date and be sure she focuses on it.

Once you have made her aware of the due date or due time or whatever the deadline is, then you have to help her set mini-deadlines. And sometimes this has to be taught over and over before she gets it.

If she has to be ready to go out the door at noon for your nephew's wedding, and if there is only one shower in the house and everybody has to use it, then teach her she has to get started a lot earlier than she would expect. She can't come waltzing in at twenty to twelve and expect to take a shower and get dressed when the rest of the family might be using that same bathroom to get ready.

Sit down with her and have her talk it through with you, starting at the final deadline (noon) and working backward, so she can figure out for herself when to get started. If she needs to wash her hair, then she can take her shower at ten and watch TV afterward if she wants. But even before that, preferably at least a day earlier, she should decide what clothes to wear or if something needs to be washed or repaired. All this has to be taken care of ahead of time. The family should not be put into a high-gear frantic panic because one child waited till the last minute and now desperately needs everyone's help to bail her out.

SCHOOL PROJECTS

The same thing goes for back-timing school projects. If a project is due at the end of the month, discuss with your child what happens when he waits till after dinner the night before the project is due to start thinking about getting his supplies and deciding what he wants to do and how he wants to do it.

He may need to collect supplies from around the neighborhood, or go shopping for tools and supplies. He has to cooperate with you and tell you ahead of time what he needs and when projects are due. In turn, whenever possible, you will cooperate with him and help him back-time until it becomes a habit and he never misses his deadlines again.

Make sure he understands that he needs to make up his own fake deadlines (the business world calls them target deadlines). Show him how to start at the real deadline and then work backward to the present. If the art project is due at the end of the month, and he estimates that it will take a couple of evenings to complete, then he had better start the project by the twenty-fifth, because he doesn't want to be schlepping it to school when the paint is still wet.

With that date set, he will have to start assembling or buying his art materials by the twenty-fourth, or at least checking to see if he has everything he needs. Show him how to make a list of what he will need, and keep reassuring him that you will work with him on the schedule this first time around.

Now if he needs someone to take him to the store, that person might not be available on the twenty-fourth, so to play it safe, he'd better start checking out art materials earlier. Your children have to realize that adults can't be expected to drop everything or leave work early just because a child has left a project until the last minute.

At first you'll have to help your children with back-timing, teaching them to talk it through and think it through. Some children find it a little difficult at first to work backward; others think it's the most natural thing in the world. I was a freshman in high school before I found out that everyone didn't read the end of a book first, or read a magazine from back to front. I just thought that's what everybody did. I naturally do things backward; back-timing was easy for me. If your child likes to think backward, he or she will love back-timing. It's the children who do things frontward who have a harder time with this. But either way, it's a fabulous habit to develop, and once children have it, it will affect many areas of their lives, and they will be so happy that you taught them this technique.

Much of this book is aimed at breaking the habit of procrastination. But with back-timing, your child is working to establish a new habit, and it might be awkward at first. Don't forget that most new habits are difficult at the beginning. When you first start learning to type or play the piano or guitar, it seems as if your fingers will never wrap around the way they are supposed to. Then the more you do it, the more natural it becomes. That's true with this habit, too. The more you back-time, the more natural and comfortable it becomes. Eventually, people just automatically think, "Okay, this is due here, let me work backward and set some target deadlines so I know when I should begin."

AT EACH STEP, A REWARD

When your child has a long-term project, such as a big-deal term paper, often the teacher will help her set a schedule: twelve weeks ahead of time do this, eleven weeks ahead of time do that. Whether the teacher or you or your child alone has set the various target deadlines, you should encourage your children to reward themselves each step of the way.

As your children develop this habit of "work hard, then reward yourself," they are learning the secret of a balanced life that many adults have never mastered. Maybe at the beginning, you are still helping with rewards, but as your children mature, help them figure out ways to provide the reward themselves. When a book report is due and your child starts reading the book well ahead of time, ask for a heads-up when she reaches the middle of the book. Offer to take her out for some small treat. Be generous with compliments, high fives, or pats on the back. Your child might treasure these as the best rewards of all.

Many parents protest against rewarding a child for setting up a schedule to do homework, then accomplishing it. They emphatically proclaim that's what the child is *supposed* to do, and it doesn't make sense to "bribe" a child for doing something he or she is supposed to be doing.

Let's not forget that these children are procrastinators who are trying to break a difficult habit and develop others that will be valuable to them all their lives in their careers, relationships, and their physical and mental health. What some parents object to as a reward or bribe, some bosses give to hardworking employees and call it a bonus or a raise. Several auto insurance companies offer a good driving discount as a reward for no traffic tickets or auto accidents. If you receive a paycheck for your job, then you are being paid for doing what you are supposed to do.

I'm not advocating that we start bribing our children, but early in the game of breaking the procrastination habit and establishing a do-it-now habit, there's nothing wrong with helping in the reward department. We're not talking about giving them a car or a trip to Europe; we're talking about small rewards of gifts or time spent with them. And what a wonderful gift you've given them, once they learn to celebrate a job well done!

The Truth Behind the Excuses

There is a great deal of shame, guilt, and anxiety associated with procrastination; your children may be making up excuses because they don't want *you* to know what they believe to be the reality: that they are incapable of doing what they want to accomplish. "I didn't have time to do my math" is easier to say than, "I don't know how to do it. I'm afraid I'm not smart enough to learn it," and "I forgot to call Grandma to ask her to buy a raffle ticket" is easier to say than, "I'm terrified to sell anything—especially this goofy raffle ticket. What if people reject me and then I start to cry?"

These young procrastinators often believe that they were born with something missing, whereas other kids can get things done. The phony excuse allows a child to avoid facing the issue and (he hopes) keeps you from knowing about this terrible flaw, or at least from discussing it.

Procrastination really does have a powerful impact on children's self-esteem and self-worth. They start to think that they aren't good enough or adequate as human beings; then the phony excuse that they don't have the time becomes a cover-up so they don't need to admit what they believe to be the real reasons—that they aren't capable of doing something, that they are too stupid or too weak or too small or too whatever. They'd prefer that others think it's a time management issue rather than what they consider to be an inadequacy issue. Fear has a lot to do with these excuses. (More on fears in chapter 7.) All of this of course is subconscious. They don't understand most of it, and are not making a conscious decision to tell a lie.

Look further into the truth within the excuses. You may find that some children simply don't care if their chores are one or their homework isn't complete. Your response then has to be, "You don't have to care. I'm not asking you to care. If you want the privilege of watching TV, get your chores done. If you want the privilege of driving a car, get your homework in on time and have it done well. That's the deal. You don't have to care."

Becky, mother of two teenage sons, both of whom stand over six-foot-six, doesn't hesitate to lay down the law to her kids, even though she's only five feet, two inches tall. "I'm not an unreasonable woman," she tells them. "I do not require you to care, or to like it. I merely require you to do it if you ever want to leave this house again." It is important to have a sense of humor, even when scolding your kids. They are less likely to tune you out if you lighten up, and they're just as apt to take you seriously.

Some parents worry, My kids don't care about anything— they have no "hot buttons," there is no reward or no privilege that would motivate them. I've never run across a single child who doesn't care about *something*. If a reward doesn't work, then losing a privilege often does. What I have seen is the child who becomes so stubborn, defiant, and resistant that she would prefer to deny that anything appeals to her rather than give an adult the satisfaction of "winning."

If you find that the real reason behind your children's excuses is that they simply don't want to do something, go back to chapter 3 and see if you can help them make the task less miserable.

EXCUSES—HABIT OR POWER PLAY?

Think about whether your child may be rebelling. When children feel powerless in a relationship or a situation, they often decide that there is too much parental control for them to argue or disobey, so they agree with you and then procrastinate. By that one act of doing nothing, they can make you crazy, enraged, or frustrated. It gives the child an odd sense of control or power, and this can start from a very young age.

The best way to handle this is to help the child gain a sense of control in his life. Talking to your child, offering helpful suggestions from this book—showing that you care—will be a great deal of help. Also, allowing the child to help make (appropriate) decisions such as what would be a good reward for this job or how he can break this chore into smaller and more manageable tasks truly helps him feel much more powerful and in control of his life.

As we explore the truth of excuses, one last area must be addressed. Does your child witness *you* saying that you don't have time to do something for her or with her, while she sees you spend time watching TV, golfing, reading, or doing some other activity more important to you than what you agreed to do? We adults certainly can get trapped by phony excuses also. Many parents find that as they help their children learn ways to blast away procrastination, they must make changes that improve their own lives as well.

As you work with helping your children eliminate old habits and establish new ways to conquer procrastination, you are building a foundation for a more productive and satisfying future for them. Their whole adult lives may be totally different because of your investment of a few months of time and energy.

TEAMWORK

Ideas to Discuss
——Why do they put off what they should be doing? How can you solve that problem?
——Back-timing.

THE NEXT STEP

Ideas in Action
——Pin them down to a specific time to do a task if they are putting you off.
——Point out phony excuses versus accepting responsibility in movies, TV shows, and so on.
——Is a dedicated study time needed in your house?
——If you suspect rebellion or a power play, help the child feel a sense of control by letting her make appropriate decisions, or selecting a priority.

6

To Be or Not to Be . . . Perfect

PERFECTIONISM AND PROCRASTINATION go hand in hand. Perfectionism is often what keeps kids from starting a project: "Everything has to be perfectly in place before I can begin."

The other side of the coin is that many perfectionists cannot end a project until everything is finished . . . well . . . perfectly. And if the project is subjective or artistic, the work is never good enough to be considered finished: "I was always fixing up my paintings, then I'd mess it up and have to start all over." Or the perfectionist will repeatedly start over again and again: "The book report will be a little late. I just have to rewrite it one more time."

Some children have enormously high expectations and standards, and become frustrated or angry easily. Often these children are also bright and creative. They're afraid of so much; the next chapter will cover specific fears, but some children's standards of perfection are not involved with specifics. The child may have many reasons for the need of perfection (usually subconscious), and he often cannot identify or discuss any of them. He may be afraid of

- hurting or disappointing parents
- losing love or respect of parents, teachers, or others
- looking bad, being bad
- not being good enough
- being made fun of
- looking foolish, stupid, or lazy
- being second-rate
- being not as good as a certain other child (sibling, cousin, neighbor)
- having weaknesses or flaws in his work or in himself

If we ask these young perfectionists *who* they are afraid will think they look bad or foolish, they don't know.

Kristin, mother of five-year-old Beth, was aware that her daughter had an "all or nothing" attitude. If she colored outside the line just a bit, Beth would become furious with herself and judge the whole page a failure. Often she'd rip the page out of her coloring book in a fury. When her mom explained that it was not worth getting angry about, Beth repeatedly responded, "Nobody will like it!"

Kristin reassured her that *she* liked it very much, and Beth insisted that nobody else would. Mom asked, "Who? Who is it that matters so much to you?" and Beth just kept saying, "Everybody."

She could never identify who "everybody" was, but whoever they were, they had enough power over Beth that she would become infuriated on a daily basis over things that were less than perfect; things that "nobody will like except Mommy." Although she feared how others would judge or criticize her, Beth was her own harshest critic. This led to Beth putting off more and more opportunities in her life because she could not accept anything of herself that she thought was less than perfect.

Sometimes little perfectionists put something off simply because no matter how often or how well they do that thing, it simply cannot meet their impossibly high expectations or their unnecessarily rigid standards. Sister Jean Frye, who has been teaching for thirty-seven years, explains, "I have run into several teens in the past who were extremely bright students, who didn't turn in their work on time and sometimes not at all. I figured out finally that they couldn't turn it in if it wasn't up to their expectations. It wasn't that they hadn't done the assignment. It just wasn't good enough by their standards."

They Don't Want to Disappoint Others

Some procrastination is based on a child wanting so badly for parents, teachers, coaches, or youth group leaders to believe she is perfect that the result is a good child who will behave in an odd or inexplicable or downright bad manner. She can't admit to making a mistake, so she lies or becomes sneaky.

When Yvonne was in junior high and high school, she was very concerned with what her parents thought of her and never wanted to let them down.

> I cared so much that I'd procrastinate in telling them bad news or sharing anything about myself that would disappoint them. An example of this is that throughout the semester when a student's grade was low, the par-

ents would have to sign the statement showing that they received the information. I would take the forms and sign my mother's name! I would do so thinking that I would get the grade back up by the end of the semester and my parents (and I) would be spared from this disappointment. Well, usually I was not able to get the grade back up, and they were disappointed anyway. They then found out that I was signing my mother's name and were also disappointed that I lied to them. They were hurt that I lied—and I didn't have the understanding of the situation at that age to explain to them that I was attempting to save them disappointment because I cared so much of what they thought of me. If I had simply given them the bad news/school grade warnings when I received them, it would have saved us all a good deal of trouble, hurt feelings, and dread.

Yvonne also says that some of her procrastination came from shyness: "I was a very shy child and probably procrastinated or just plain avoided altogether many situations and opportunities."

Hugo described his thirteen-year-old son, Luis: "Whether it's sports, schoolwork, playing the trumpet, everything—he doesn't think in terms of success; instead, he's motivated by fear of failure—which he considers to be anything less than perfect. Since he was little he seemed to measure his sense of self-worth by what he does or accomplishes, and he is always angry or frustrated because what he does just isn't 'good enough.' Then, when he does a great job, there doesn't seem to be any pleasure in it, because it is simply what he expected. He looks . . . empty."

Hugo's wife, Yolanda, continued, "Our friends tell us that Luis being a perfectionist is nothing compared to their children's struggles with grades or apathy toward work. Our neighbor always says that this should be our worst problem, then we'd never have a worry in our lives. Many people don't fully appreciate how limiting and even debilitating perfectionism can be. They just don't get it."

WHY DO CHILDREN BECOME PERFECTIONISTS?

Judith Starkey, a professional speaker in Illinois and authority on cultural influences, says that she looks back at her childhood and recognizes that those times she procrastinated were invariably due to perfectionism that stemmed from "fear of failure, fear of not living up to expectations, always wanting to excel, never wanting to make a mistake. It is safer to do nothing, but also far less rewarding."

I doubt if anyone knows all the reasons why a person becomes a perfectionist. Many parents insist that their child was born this way, and they tell stories of their child before he was two, getting frustrated because he couldn't meet his incredibly high standards while playing with his building blocks. Other parents look back to their child's earlier years and insist that they can spot just where the child's feelings of not being "good enough" started.

Rebecca said that when her children were little, if they made their beds, cleared off the table, or wiped up spilled milk, she would often do it over. Her sister criticized Rebecca for taking away the children's sense of pride and accomplishment, but Rebecca explained that this is how they learn to do the job with better results. Then one day Rebecca and her husband were rototilling the soil in the corner of their backyard to prepare it for planting a garden. Rebecca said she raked and raked until the soil was perfectly smooth and there were no clumps in it. Then as she stood back to admire all her hard work, her husband picked up the rake and reraked the whole garden.

Rebecca said, "I was devastated. I worked so hard and was so proud of myself, and without saying a word, he redid the whole thing as if *nothing* was right. I wanted to wrap that rake around his neck, and I decided then and there that I would never, ever rake that garden again.

"But in that instant, I also understood how my kids must feel when I redo their work, *and* I understood why they now hate doing all the chores that I redo. From that day on, I've never, ever done any of their work over again. But already, two of my three children believed that what they do is never good enough, and they would do their homework over and over, and *still* not hand it in."

Bridget, in discussing her ten-year-old son Pat, said, "He defines who he is by what he does and how well he does it. His self-worth is based entirely on his ability to do something. So sometimes he decides that if he never finishes the job, then the world can never judge his ability . . . or inability." She had heard that children need encouragement rather than praise, and she could never figure out the difference. Then one day Pat was making some bookends out of wood, and Bridget walked by and said, "You're a terrific woodworker, Pat." He said, "No, I'm not," and in a fury closed everything down. And he never finished those bookends.

She had been trying to help Pat understand that the process of learning and the enjoyment of achievement are much more important than getting the highest grades in his class. So she tried to apply this idea (of encouraging him) to his woodworking. Next time she saw him making something, she said, "You seem to really enjoy this work, don't you, Pat?" He chatted with her a while, and she realized that talking about how much he enjoyed the work was, to Pat, an "acceptable" compliment. But to praise him and call him a terrific woodworker gave him a standard that he didn't even want to try to live up to.

So the question is, Why do children become perfectionists? Well, after talking to hundreds of parents and therapists from all over the world, the inevitable conclusion is—nobody knows.

How Can We Help a Perfectionist?

There's lots of advice out there about teaching the perfectionist deep breathing exercises or to count to ten when he starts to feel angry or frustrated. I don't disagree with these ideas, but I believe it makes more sense to start off explaining to him how perfectionism can be counterproductive. It usually causes procrastination and stress, neither of which is compatible with high standards of achievement.

Often these children don't realize there are other options when they want to do a great job. They confuse a standard of perfection—if something isn't perfect, it's worthless—with a standard of excellence that values high-quality results. What they don't realize is that excellence is achievable; perfection seldom is.

What a great gift it would be to the whole family to have a family discussion (in the car, at dinner, in any relaxed atmosphere) about the difference between a standard of excellence and a standard of perfection. You could tell them where you stand on this issue.

Sometimes children observe perfectionist behavior in

someone else in the family. (Could it possibly be you?) If you do have this struggle, you could share with them times that your perfectionism got you in trouble, and how instead an expectation of excellence could have helped the situation.

Darlene told her children the story of how she had been writing a thank-you note to a friend, when she was interrupted by something that caused her to make a mistake, which she crossed out. Then she decided that the crossed-out mistake looked messy, so she put it aside to rewrite the note someday when she would have a chunk of time free of interruptions. She never got around to sending that thank-you note.

About a year later, she received a note from another friend that brightened up her whole day. When she read it a second time, she noticed that one word had been crossed out and rewritten. Darlene thought to herself, Isn't it better to receive an imperfect note (with one word crossed out) that brings me joy than not to receive a note at all—perfect or otherwise?

If you have a story of how perfectionism caused you problems, you can share it with your family.

Oops! I Made a Mistake

Have you lived long enough to know that many of the biggest lessons that you've learned in life have come from making mistakes? With a constructive attitude, you can learn from a mistake and move on. But if your attitude is, "Ohhhh nooooo, I've made a mistake. What a miserable, worthless worm am I," then you learn nothing, and often you put off anything that might result in a mistake—including potentially wonderful activities and experiences.

Share with your children this story of what Mario learned

by reading biographies. His favorite part was when the central character of the book made a mistake or experienced failure. He said, "No matter who your favorite hero or heroine is, he or she has experienced huge mistakes and failures. And the more successful they are, the more mistakes they've made.

"According to a biography of Lincoln that I just read, before being elected president, Lincoln lost several elections, had a serious relationship end, and was hospitalized for depression. Yet he went on to become a great and popular president."

When you discuss mistakes with your young perfectionist, or hopefully with the whole family, let them know how you feel when you make a mistake. Do you fall apart and berate yourself, or do you figure out what you can learn from it and move on? If you are struggling to handle mistakes in a positive way, share your struggles with your family. Ask them,

- What are acceptable ways to handle mistakes in your family?
- What are appropriate reactions to mistakes?
- Have you, or any family member, ever learned something from making a mistake?
- Regardless of what has happened in the past, can you as a family decide to allow mistakes to happen and accept them as a normal part of life?

Once we can accept and live with our own mistakes, it is often easier to accept the mistakes of others. It mainly comes down to accepting that *all* humans make mistakes; you can either become miserable over mistakes, or you can use them as a learning lesson.

IDENTIFYING SELF-TALK

Most of our reactions to mistakes come from our self-talk. When your young perfectionist gets angry or frustrated with something that is less than perfect, she often believes that she can't help feeling what she feels. But feelings come from our thoughts, and our thoughts are based on our self-talk.

Only your child can know what she is saying to herself, but often even *she* is unaware of her self-talk (because it is usually subconscious) when she experiences imperfection. But you can help her try to figure it out. You can tell your children what some of your self-talk is when you make a mistake. For example, you may be working on going from "I am so stupid" to "That may have been a dumb mistake, but I'm still a smart person." Also, you can suggest a variety of possible negative messages that might be part of your child's subconscious self-talk, and let her figure out if that might be what she is saying to herself. Some of these negative messages might be:

- Everybody must love and approve of me at all times.
- I must be competent and perfect in everything I do.
- If people disapprove of me, it means I'm wrong or bad or not good enough.
- My worth as a person depends on how much I achieve and produce.

Little Beth, the five-year-old who in a fury ripped pages out of her coloring book when her pictures weren't perfect, was possibly saying to herself, "I colored outside the line, and now the whole picture is ruined, and nobody ever will like it." Kristen can help her change that message by repeatedly encouraging her to say, "I colored outside the line, but the rest of the picture looks pretty good, and I really enjoy coloring. It's fun." As you work with your child, you can point out how negative self-talk really sabotages any fun and sense of joy or achievement.

Yvonne, who signed her mother's name on the notes from school, might have been telling herself, "If my parents find out about my low grades, it will devastate them and ruin their lives, and they probably won't love me anymore." Sometimes, as we uncover our own or our children's self-talk, it sounds pretty exaggerated and melodramatic, but often that is the way we subconsciously talk to ourselves, and it gets us in all kinds of trouble and causes unhappiness. Yvonne could change that message to, "When my parents find out about my low grades, they will be very disappointed. They may punish me or insist I work harder. Well, at least they'll know the truth, and I won't feel guilty and like a liar and a sneak."

Trying to figure out self-talk can be difficult at first, but once a person starts to unravel the mystery, it becomes an amazing journey. As your child works to change her self-talk and realizes that her feelings change (including her feelings about herself and her self-worth), she will probably start to experience less stress and more joy and her procrastination will begin to diminish.

WOULD THE PERFECT PARENT PLEASE STAND UP?

Linda Brakeall, a professional speaker and the author of *Unlocking the Secrets of Successful Women in Business*, says, "It is totally unreasonable to expect to be a perfect or even a competent parent at every phase of your child's life. You may be a great parent with your babies, and fall apart when they hit adolescence. Or great with teenagers but distant and 'absent' with toddlers. Each stage of a child's development requires different parenting skills. It's silly to believe that you'll excel through every stage with every child. Some people do, but not everyone."

I agree. There actually *was* a time I when was a perfect parent, and I knew all the answers—then the first baby came along, and suddenly I realized I didn't even know what the questions were.

If our children get into trouble expecting perfection, so do we.

- Are you expecting yourself to be a perfect parent or teacher or grandparent, or whatever your relationship is with this child?
- Are you expecting yourself to have all the answers? (Nobody else does, you know.)
- Are you expecting yourself to teach your child every single thing in this book?
- Are you expecting your child to accept your teaching and change instantly, and for you all to live happily ever after? (Does the term *fairy tale* come to mind?)

It's okay if you've tried to teach them something and it didn't go over well. You never know what your children might pick up just by *you* understanding or doing something in a new or different way.

Maybe you haven't begun talking to your children about procrastination yet. You never know, maybe—just maybe—one day you'll say to yourself, "I don't have to wait for the perfect time or the right conditions or situation till my kids are in a perfect mood or whatever, I'm in the mood to talk about procrastination right now."

What you decide to say does not have to be perfect. So relax and trust yourself.

TEAMWORK

Ideas to Discuss

——If your child has perfectionist tendencies, it's important to have some discussions with him. If you can help turn his attitudes around, his life will be so much happier and easier.

——Understand that a standard of perfection leads to procrastination and stress. Is that part of their expectation of themselves?

——Excellence is achievable; perfection is seldom achievable.

——It's okay to make a mistake. We can learn from it. (Tell about mistakes made by Abraham Lincoln or other successful people.)

——Share how you handle mistakes.

——What are acceptable ways to handle mistakes in your family?

——Self-talk leads to thoughts, thoughts lead to feelings.

——Share any of your own self-talk that you've uncovered, especially if it has to do with perfection or making mistakes.

——Offer to help your child come up with a message to override any negative ones. (Change "Nobody will love me if I make a mistake" to "Oops! I made a mistake so I better see what I can learn from it.")

Ideas in Action

——Decide if you can accept excellence instead of perfection from your child.

——As a team, list the positives and negatives of making a mistake.

110 • THE PROCRASTINATING CHILD

7

The Fear Factor of
Procrastination

ONE OF THE MORE SUBTLE CAUSES of procrastination is fear,
which can lurk in our subconscious and has the power to immobilize us. Sometimes people, including kids, put something off for weeks or months because of some unknown,
unidentified fear; yet once that fear is recognized and has a
name, the procrastination often disappears without our
working on or struggling with it.

The first step is to uncover any fears that have caused you
to procrastinate, and share them with your children. It will
help them be more open to identifying their own fears. The
place to start identifying your child's fears is a conversation
about what the child is putting off and what might be the fear
behind it. Help him talk about it and try to uncover what he
might be afraid of that is holding him back.

As long as their fears are subconscious, your children not
only won't know what the fears are, they won't even know
that the fears exist. And whenever that is the case, those fears
will have tremendous power over your children. What are
these fears? In the previous chapter, we already explored fear

of being imperfect, which includes fear of not being good enough, fear of making a mistake, and fear of disappointing someone or of someone not approving of you. We also discussed fear of failure, something that everyone seems to understand—but what about fear of success?

FEAR OF SUCCESS

The idea of success can terrify a child. Think about it. Of course, it's not true of all schools, but in many schools, success is not considered cool. If you are smart, you are probably thought of as a geek; if you are a hard worker, you are often called teacher's pet. The only ones who experience some sort of popularity with their success are the athletes and the cheerleaders.

Not only might children sometimes believe success is bad, they may fear the expectations that might accompany success. Andy remembers sitting in the backyard with his folks when he was about eight years old. "Our neighbor had just received a huge promotion at work, and my dad said, 'Now he'll probably be too big for his britches. He'll drive a big, flashy car and will think he's too good to talk to us.' On some level I decided that success turned us into bad, lonely people who were too mean to ever have friends. And I knew I never wanted to be too big for my britches, whatever that meant."

Many children do believe that success has a negative impact on a person—they think people who succeed financially are mean, arrogant, conceited, divorced, lonely, and their children hate them. In a child's mind, success could mean skipping a grade or being moved to an honors class, maybe to a different school. That means change and the unknown— leaving old friends and comfortable ways.

Some children fear that if they succeed at something, then they will be expected to do it again. What if they can't? And some children fear success because it means people will pay lots of attention to them and look at them, and they really don't want to be singled out.

Many children of all ages think of success as very scary. Any time someone sets a goal and then starts sabotaging himself or shooting himself in the foot, it's time to suspect that fear of success is at work.

Fear of the Unknown or of Change

Change is one of the biggest causes of stress. It's scary and feels chaotic because we have so little control during times of change. And yet many say that the only constant that we will experience in life is change.

Our children are living through change at a far more rapid rate than we ever did when we were their age. But when they are putting off filing their college application or meeting new friends, they often are clueless about how much power fear of the unknown and fear of change hold over them.

Dawdling before going someplace, even a familiar place, is sometimes a sign of fear in a young child. The child feels safe and comfortable at home, and puts off packing up to go to Grandma's house because he never knows who will be there to play with, or whether that uncle who teases him will be there.

When children put off getting ready to leave for some new place such as a new day-care center or school, don't nag them. Instead you might have more success helping them with information about the "unknown." Taking them for a visit ahead of time helps, or at least offering answers about what will they eat, how can they find the bathrooms, what they are supposed to do if another child bullies them, what they do if they feel sick, and how they can reach you if they need you.

Rather than be frightened of the unknown, many children would prefer to discuss subjects that we think would frighten them. When six-year-old Wendy's mom died, all through the wake and funeral, she kept asking everyone who would listen to her what would happen if her dad died. Everyone reassured her that her daddy wasn't going to die, but Wendy kept asking.

Finally an aunt sat down with her and told her that Wendy would come to live at her aunt's house. Wendy then had a dozen questions; obviously she had given this a great deal of thought. Would she have to share a bedroom with her cousin? What would happen to her old house? Would she have to change her last name? What grade would she be in if she had to change schools? Could she continue taking skating lessons? Could she come back and visit her old friends? What would happen to their dog and two cats?

Her aunt couldn't possibly know all these answers, but she recognized Wendy's need to be reassured, so she answered as best she could. She admits that she just made up some answers and fudged others. For example, the idea of adding Wendy's three pets to the zoo already living in her house seemed impossible, but she was not about to tell that to a six-year-old at her mommy's wake, so the aunt said of course Wendy's dog and two cats would join her family. This aunt's reassurance about the unknown was all that little child needed, and she finally stopped asking about what would happen if her daddy died.

If you suspect that fear of change or of the unknown is

causing your children to procrastinate, share with them times when you dreaded a change, and it turned out to be something wonderful. When Sue Lin couldn't get any of her four children to start packing up their toys and "stuff" for the big move to a new house, Sue Lin opened a discussion about change. She told them how resistant she had been years earlier to learning to work on a computer. All four kids roared with laughter at the idea of anyone not knowing how to work a computer.

Sue Lin took the kidding good-naturedly, and they all talked for a minute or two about times they were afraid of the unknown or of change. That conversation, plus a firm promise that they would all be able to return frequently to visit friends in the old neighborhood, seemed to relieve the fear that was keeping them from packing. They finally took the packing boxes that Sue Lin had deposited in their rooms weeks earlier and started filling them up.

If you can't give your children more information about the unknown (sometimes you don't know any more than they do), at least talk to them about how normal it is to be afraid of change and the unknown. Most people feel better after simply talking about their fears.

FEAR OF BEING JUDGED, CRITICIZED, OR PUNISHED

This is often what is behind our fear of making a mistake. Like little Beth tearing out coloring book pages in the previous chapter, we often don't have any idea who might be in a position to judge, criticize, or punish us, but we fear them just the same.

This fear also is often behind a child's shyness. Rather than risk being criticized, the child backs off and doesn't want to "perform" or greet a guest or talk to company or do anything that might lead to judgment. So he also puts off making new friends or trying new opportunities.

When a child does not have a clear idea of what is expected or of how the authority figure will judge his behavior, fear of criticism prompts the child to put off acting on what his heart tells him to do. A child might want to express some feeling to a teacher, a youth-group leader, or another adult, but holds back for fear of judgment—from the adult or from the other kids.

When Randy was a teenager, he wanted to congratulate a classmate's mother, Mrs. Coleman, who he spotted at a church function. Randy had known Mrs. Coleman since kindergarten, because she would accompany the class on field trips and help out at class parties. He wasn't close to her, but he liked her and knew she'd just had a book published. He was dying to talk to her because Randy, too, wanted to be an author, and his mom had just bought Mrs. Coleman's book. Still, he kept finding excuses not to go up and talk to her. Yet he kept thinking about it and glancing at her out of the corner of his eye.

He was mad at himself for being a coward and not talking to her, but nothing he said to himself could budge him out of his procrastination. Finally, at the end of the evening, another teenager walked up to her and congratulated her. She smiled, thanked him graciously, and chatted with him a moment. As Randy watched, he thought to himself, "That looks easy. I can do that." And he did!

All he needed was to see someone else model the behavior; then he was able to do the same thing. When we recognize this fear in children, helping them see how someone else does something or describing clear expectations, or even helping them practice greeting people or shaking hands with an authority figure, can sometimes enable them to move out of their procrastinating mode and dive into what they've been wanting to do all along.

Fear of Too Much Responsibility

This could be a spinoff of fear of success. We fear that if we succeed, we are responsible for maintaining that level of success. The child subconsciously wonders, Does doing something that I've been putting off raise other people's expectations of me?

Ryan told about how his son Zak worked hard at his studies, but usually pulled grades of C, seldom higher. Then the summer between sixth and seventh grade, something happened. Perhaps Zak simply matured or his attention span increased because of a new video game they bought, or if it's possible, maybe he outgrew a learning disability.

Whatever it was, when he went back to school he worked as hard as he always did, but with surprisingly different results. He made the honor roll! Yet when he handed his report card to his parents, Zak had such a discouraged look on his face, they both thought that he was failing everything. His mom was the first to realize what happened; she shouted, "Zak, you made the honor roll!" With a look of sincere concern, Zak answered, "Yes, but please don't expect me to do it again."

Sadly, adults as well as children often put off doing things because they fear that success will burden them with more responsibility than they can handle.

Fear of Anticipated Feelings

Odd as it may seem, many people put off doing something not because they know how they would feel doing it, but because they fear how they *might* feel as the result of doing it. They might feel stupid, embarrassed, ugly, foolish, anything.

It sounds like a trivial or silly reason to procrastinate, but this fear can hold a powerful grip on a person, keeping him frozen in place, unable to move forward in the direction he has chosen, and it maintains that grip as long as it remains subconscious. But simply bringing it forward, identifying it, or giving it a name can knock out any power that fear held over a person.

Once a child realizes that the fear of feeling stupid was what held her in its grip, the child often laughs at how silly it was to put off something just because she was afraid of a potential—not even a real—feeling. Especially if she is confident that she is not stupid.

Sometimes when we are terrified of doing something, we have to go ahead and do it even though we're scared. Rachel told the story of how as a child she was scared of everything. She never wanted to do anything, and her repeated mantra was, "I'd be too afraid to do that," or "I can't do that. It's too scary." Finally, her father decided that her life was turning into one big prison of fear, so he started telling her, "Maybe you'll feel scared, and maybe you won't. If you do, go ahead and do it scared." His message was always the same; he just kept changing the feelings. "Maybe you'll feel self-conscious, and maybe not. If you do, go ahead and do it even if you feel self-conscious."

He taught Rachel that it was okay to experience feelings. Today Rachel is a bold woman who runs her own business and takes risks constantly. She thanks her dad for helping her get past her fear of feelings when she was little.

FEAR OF REJECTION

Most of us have experienced at some time during our childhood the dread of selling something for a fund-raiser at school. This dread stems from fear of rejection, even if your parents are only urging you to call Grandma. Yet most grandmothers are pushovers who would buy anything from you, whether she needed it or not. But most kids have to be pushed—kicking and screaming—into asking people to buy from them, and their idea of huge success is when they "con" Mom or Dad into buying up everything they are selling. When we help a child overcome this fear (instead of bailing him out) and teach him to risk rejection—even if he feels scared—we are teaching him a skill that will serve him well on many levels for the rest of his life.

We also witness this fear of rejection in children regarding their relationships. Taking the risk of asking a girl out can be terrifying to a teenage boy, and how many kids of all ages eat alone in the lunchroom rather than go up to a table full of kids and ask to join them?

Everybody knows that rejection will not hurt us physically, but the potential for receiving it can create as much fear as the threat of being tossed out of a plane without a parachute.

An odd spinoff of this is fear of imposing. Some children are so convinced that whatever they request will be so inconvenient, such an imposition, that they can never ask for what they want. They'll hint or giggle or sometimes whisper to someone else, but they just can't come out and say, "May I please have something to drink?"

It's important that we help children past this fear, because otherwise they expect people to have a crystal ball and read their minds to know what they need or want. Then, when people fail to guess their needs, these children (and some adults, too) feel unloved and unappreciated. This is not good for a child, not good for an adult, and terrible for communication in any relationship. If children don't learn to ask politely for a glass of water when they are little, then they don't ask for what they want in relationships when they are older. This causes all kinds of crazy miscommunications.

We have to teach children when they are young that it is okay to politely ask for what they need or want. Point out to them how you do it, and help them understand that not everybody in this world is going to give us what we ask for, but that does not mean that we have imposed, nor does it mean we have been personally rejected.

FEAR OF MAKING THE WRONG DECISION

You may not think that children have many important decisions to make, yet many of their decisions are very important to them. This fear grabs kids when they are overwhelmed. They just can't decide where to start. For example, they'll put off doing homework, and we think they are lazy or unmotivated or being rebellious, and it all comes down to the fact that they can't decide what subject to do first. If they finally do make that decision, then they don't know where to start within that subject. The whole evening passes by, and they never started, because they never decided.

The child who fears making important decisions may also struggle with simple decisions, such as what to order at a restaurant. Children need to gain confidence in their decision-making abilities and overcome their fear that living with the results of their decision will be worse than the misery of indecisiveness and procrastination.

When a fear really has hold of your child, help him learn to confront the fear by exaggerating it or ballooning it. Sometimes the wilder the exaggeration, the better. Ask your child to think of what would happen if his worst fears came true. He would not be happy if someone criticized something he'd done or if he were rejected, but he wouldn't die from it. He might feel bad for a while, but doesn't he feel bad when he's procrastinating about whatever it is he's supposed to do?

For example, if the child is struggling to decide what to order at a restaurant, ask him what would happen if he got served the most rotten and most disgusting meal in the world. Help him brainstorm answers.

- Would he have to starve to death if he missed one meal?

- Would other members of the family share some of their meal with him?
- Would he be allowed to send it back?
- Would he be punished or scolded? (This could be the key to a child's fear. Is he afraid you'll say, "You ordered it. Now you have to eat it whether you like it or not!")

When your daughter has a hard time getting dressed in the morning and you suspect that it's because she's afraid of making the wrong decision, ask her what would happen if she picked out the ugliest outfit in the world.

- Would someone make fun of the way she's dressed? Her siblings? Friends at school? You?
- If she doesn't realize until she gets to school that she's wearing the world's ugliest outfit, can she survive the day?
- If she realized the mistake before leaving the house, would she have time to change?
- Would you tell her the outfit wasn't working and offer to help her select a better outfit?
- Would you force her to wear the ugly outfit all day long? (This might be what caused the fear in the first place: "You picked it out, now you wear it!")

Ballooning fears is a simple little exercise that can become a lifelong habit helping your children get past the stranglehold that fears have on them. Another way you can help is by giving your children appropriate decisions to make, such as what they want to eat or to wear. Don't burden them with decisions that are too difficult or too serious for their age. Children can also benefit from learning not to second-guess their decisions.

Justin has taught his daughters a valuable quick decision-making skill: he tells them to decide to act and not look back.

Helping your children understand and identify fears at any age will be a helpful habit for them all their lives. As you read this, did you recognize any times that fear of something caused you to procrastinate? These fears may be subtle, but once your child learns to uncover them, they will no longer hold any power over her. Sometimes, just identifying them eliminates much of the procrastination in someone's life.

TIPS TO SHARE WITH YOUR CHILD

~~~~~

This **HIVE** *will help conquer that fear that is causing you to procrastinate.*

Have a conversation; talking about a fear helps move it from the subconscious to the conscious mind, and reduces its power over you.

Identify the fear; give it a name.

View it simply as a feeling; if you procrastinate because you feel scared, go ahead and do it scared.

Exaggerate the fear; balloon it. What's the worst that could happen?

TEAMWORK

Ideas to Discuss

——Times that a fear caused me to procrastinate.

——How fears can immobilize us until we bring them to our conscious mind by naming them:

——Fear of being imperfect

——Fear of being not good enough

————Fear of making a mistake
————Fear of disappointing someone (or losing their approval)
————Fear of failure
————Fear of success
————Fear of the unknown or of change
————Fear of being judged, criticized, or punished
————Fear of too much responsibility
————Fear of feelings
————Fear of being rejected
————Fear of making the wrong decision
————Ballooning a fear. Give examples. Help them establish this habit.

THE NEXT STEP

Ideas in Action
————Stop being afraid to talk to your children about what you are learning in this book. By the way, what *are* you afraid of?

8

"Let My Clutter Go"

When it's time for children to put something away, they tend to head in one of two directions. The first is that they put it where it belongs, and are done with it. End of story.

The second is:

- they put off deciding whether to get rid of it or keep it.
- if they've decided to keep it, they procrastinate in deciding when and where to put it away; or
- they know the time to put it away is *now*, and they know *where* it goes, but they just procrastinate in putting it where it belongs.

The result of going in this second direction is clutter.

Since children of today have more "stuff" to clutter up their world than previous generations did, clutter can become a huge problem for many children. They live in chaos and can never find what they need. Your gift to them will be to teach them how to organize and manage the clutter coming into their lives so that they can develop into functional, effective people.

There are some children, however, who have so much clutter that nobody can see a surface—none of the floor shows, not one portion of any dresser top is in view—yet these children will be able to find and quickly put their hands on anything they're looking for. It's as if they know where everything is, even though you can't walk through all the piles of stuff. This ability is *not* a good enough excuse to keep all that clutter.

Sometimes children procrastinate in trying to detach from something. They no longer love it or want it, but for some reason, they feel attached to old stuff, perhaps because they think they *should* keep this thing, or it's wrong to get rid of it. Teach your sentimental children that nobody has to be keeper of *everything*, and that life will go on if they get rid of it.

If children can learn to decide immediately what to do about a toy, a book, a piece of paper, an E-mail, then act on that decision by either getting rid of it or putting it where it belongs, they will eliminate most of their clutter. Helping children gain control of their clutter falls into four steps: Meet the Clutter BUGS.

TIPS TO SHARE WITH YOUR CHILD

~~~~~~

Let the Clutter BUGS *help you.*
Break now the habit of "Save, collect, and keep."
Undertake some action—don't leave things in a heap.
Get rid of stuff that clutters up your brain.
Stop bringing in more clutter that starts it all again.

Children often accumulate clutter because they put off:

- sorting through and organizing it.
- deciding what to do with it.
- getting rid of it.
- saying no to bringing more clutter into their lives.
- a commitment to not shop for or buy more clutter.

When a Collection Becomes Clutter

It seems as if the minute children say, "I love trains" (or stuffed animals, or *Sesame Street*, or unicorns, or Mickey Mouse, or Beanie Babies, or dinosaurs, or whatever), their loving, adoring family begins to shower them with these items. In no time, the child is buried under tons of stuff he collects, and he is so overwhelmed, he can't keep up with it all. Or her room is bursting at the seams with her collection, and she feels swamped just trying to find a place for her other things and keep her collection looking clean (or at least not looking like dust balls).

Sometimes the children never even wanted to be collectors. All they did was put a cute little statue of a monkey on a shelf, and family members or friends decided, "By Jove, *now* I know what to buy for the next birthday present!" And in the blink of an eye, the child becomes the proud owner of a trailer truck-load of monkeys. And eventually, there are so many monkeys that he can't enjoy looking at the one that started it all, the one he really loves, because he can't even find it.

If a collection is a true source of joy to the child, you love giving it space and caring for it because it also gives you joy, and there is no problem, then leave it alone. It's not considered clutter. Enjoy.

However, if your child loved these things once but now doesn't pay any attention to them, or worse yet, is annoyed by trying to keep them looking nice or trying to work around them, it's time to make a decision about this collection. Usually, it's not the getting rid of the collectibles that the child procrastinates about; what is most often put off is deciding to stop collecting or what to do with the collected items that now have become so troublesome.

BREAK THE HABIT OF COLLECTING THINGS YOU NO LONGER WANT

Children can break the collecting habit in a number of ways.

Debra's daughter Taylor had a penguin collection that was a delight for about three years, then just turned into a big bother. These itty-bitty black-and-white statues overflowed her shelves and her dresser and, as Taylor said, were becoming junky. She said her room looked like a Penguins R Us store, and there was no space to put anything else, including her schoolbooks. Taylor asked for more places to put her penguins, but Debra felt that was unreasonable.

> When you don't have room for all your stuff, you don't need more room, you need less stuff.

Then Debra walked her daughter through the house to show her that there was no other place to put the collection without making *that* place look cluttered and junky as well. Debra suggested that the penguins had served their purpose;

they had provided happiness and pleasure for a long time, and now it was time for them to "retire." Taylor agreed.

Often a child who is resistant to getting rid of a collection gets to this stage, realizes that the house does not have unlimited space to accommodate his stuff, and finally accepts the fact that something has to go.

This was a decision that deep in her heart, Taylor probably already knew, but she would have procrastinated in thinking about it and deciding about it without her mother's coaching.

UNDERTAKE SOME ACTION

Sometimes to simply stop collecting is enough, but often it is not: Something has to be done with the existing collection. To just let it sit there still annoying your child (and maybe even you) hasn't solved anything. Don't make your children live with clutter if they are ready to say good-bye to it. They deserve better than that. But most kids do need help from you in getting rid of things that they once loved. They need help to let go emotionally, and they need help now taking action to pack away or to deliver these collections to where they belong. This step is where most children will procrastinate unless they receive strong support and guidance from you.

Debra and Taylor came up with a plan: Taylor would select a few favorites to pack away and save, then they would give away the rest. Although she was allowed to save as many penguins as she wanted to, Debra estimates it was less than one-tenth of the collection. Taylor really was ready to let go of these little critters.

Then she had a great time wrapping up the remainder of the penguins and giving them away to friends, neighbors, a favorite school secretary, her doctor, and the grocery store lady who was always nice to her.

Help children not only to select what goes out (maybe all of the collection, or maybe a portion of it) but also to pack it up and bring it to where they and you have decided it will go. Debra helped Taylor pack up a portion of her penguins, provided paper to wrap the giveaways, and reminded her to bring some with her when they visited neighbors or went to the doctor or grocery store.

GET RID OF IT

Many children are willing to relinquish their collection as long as it's not going into the garbage. Sentimental children become heartbroken if they have to throw out something that was once cherished. Most children cannot do that. Truthfully, most adults cannot do that.

Your challenge is to find ways of getting rid of their cherished stuff without throwing it away. Share with children what you do when you have too many books or audio- or videotapes cluttering up your life. How do you select what goes? What do you do with it? (If you just live with it because you can't part with any of it, perhaps you should share with them a different area of clutter in your life—hopefully one you've succeeded in managing.)

Children usually are less likely to procrastinate and more willing to let go of their treasures if they know that someone else will cherish and value them. You could help your children take collections of things such as stuffed animals or comic books and pass them on to other, less fortunate children. That way, they not only declutter their lives, they also will have learned about helping people in need. This involves finding a place to bring it. Probably a call to a local family service agency, church, synagogue, or your city hall clerk would give you some leads.

If your child is very sentimental and cannot part with his collection, you and he could pack the entire collection away with hopes he'll find enjoyment in it again at another time. Put it in the attic, basement, garage, or someplace else safe.

SELECT A PLACE FOR EVERYTHING

If your child finds his collection annoying but simply cannot get rid of it or pack it away, make an effort to find a manageable way to display it so that it will not collect dust or be knocked over by the cats or take up valuable space that he would like to use for something else. Sometimes a bookcase or shelves hung on the wall help to solve the problem.

Ivan hung a net in the upper corner of his son's room for all his stuffed animals. Once his son finally had a place to put his collection and he could see all of it, he decided to select the nicest-looking ones and was willing to give away the older, more faded ones.

Julia bought a bookcase with glass doors to display her daughter's doll collection. It was a wonderful solution; the dolls were displayed nicely so everyone could see them, yet the glass doors kept them from turning into dust-catchers.

Jasmine's daughter wanted to collect comic books, but the books didn't have a place. So they wound up all over the house, eventually getting ripped or damaged. And like any comic book collector, Jasmine's daughter would be furious if her comics were "destroyed" by her younger brothers. So Jasmine brought home a box from work, and her daughter saved money to buy plastic sleeves for each book. Then she was able to store the box in her closet, and even to neatly file and categorize her beloved comic books.

These three children enjoyed having their collections on display, and as they helped to set up the display, each of them became more selective. Once they could see all of their collections, they each were willing to throw out or pass on items that were not great looking to them.

STOP BRINGING IN MORE CLUTTER THAT STARTS IT ALL AGAIN

After a child has selected what to keep on display, what to pack away, what to get rid of, and how to get rid of it, there is one more step to take. Without it, the clutter starts all over again. The child—usually with your guidance—has to figure out a way to stop bringing in more collectibles. If procrastination puts off this decision, the clutter simply starts all over again.

The most obvious solution is to stop buying the items that have become so overwhelming, but what does the child do about all those loving friends and family who have been showering her with all her collectibles? Taylor, who had grown tired of her penguin collection, did not have a hard time packing them away or giving them away as gifts to special people. She didn't have a hard time *deciding* to call her friends and relatives and tell them that she no longer collected penguins. But the procrastination set in when it was time to make those calls. Finally, her mother Debra made a deal with her. Taylor would make the first call to the "easiest person," and if that person's reaction was upsetting to Taylor, Debra would make the remaining calls.

Weeks before her next birthday, Taylor called her favorite aunt and recited the "speech" she had practiced with her mom: "I don't collect penguins anymore, but don't worry, I've packed some away, and I'm not sure, but I think all the ones you gave me are in there. Do you want to know what I want for this coming birthday?"

She was proud of herself for making a call that had seemed scary at first, and after that she made one more call. Then she asked Debra to help bail her out and finish the calling. Debra felt that Taylor had done a terrific job in making decisions and following through, and she was going to be talking to most of the family before Taylor's next birthday anyway, so she offered to "spread the word" that Taylor no longer collected penguins.

For some people this will work, and their loving, adoring family will cooperate; for some it won't. My husband is a train nut, and out of our nine grandchildren, just one, Connor Patrick, is also a train nut. If someday Connor outgrows trains and asks Grandpa to stop with the trains, I have a feeling the trains won't stop. Actually, I suspect that if some day Connor is president of the United States or a Nobel Peace Prize winner, he will still be receiving Thomas the Tank engines from Grandpa ChooChoo.

Collections are wonderful; children learn from them and derive great comfort and enjoyment from them. Collections only become clutter when they are through serving their purpose, children no longer enjoy them, and they are taking up valuable room needed for other purposes.

GENERAL CLUTTER

In addition to collections, children have an abundance of general clutter filling up their rooms, overflowing their closets and dresser drawers, and often scattered around the house. It accumulates because they have either procrastinated in deciding whether to keep something, procrastinated in deciding where and when to put it away, or simply procrastinated in putting it away.

There are so many reasons people keep clutter. Ask your children if they know why. Sometimes asking a group of kids questions such as, "Who has too much stuff? Who has stuff you don't need cluttering up your life? Do you know why you keep it all?" can lead to interesting insights for them *and* you. Your child won't feel picked on or defensive because the topic is not aimed at him; it involves the whole group.

Ingrid, the mother of two teens and a grade-schooler, said that her favorite place to have this kind of conversation is while driving someplace with a van full of kids, and one question that brought some lively discussion during "car communication" was, "Do you really want to be the caretaker of all that junk?" She now has asked that question several times, and has heard answers that are often funny and sometimes poignant.

"Impossible. There's too much junk to take care of."

"I think the junk takes care of me, or at least it seems to control me."

"No, but nobody is caretaker of anything in our house. Stuff just piles up everywhere."

"No, I don't want to be caretaker of all that junk, but what can I do?"

She says many replies express helplessness, as if it's a battle with the clutter, and the clutter is stronger.

She also asks kids, "If somebody gives you something, does that mean you have to keep it?" and has been surprised that every one of them has said that yes, they had to keep it, or it would hurt the giver's feelings.

She suggested a compromise: Keep it for a while, then pack it away, give it away, or throw it away; almost any giver would understand that we might use something for a while and then move on.

Once a boy way in the backseat said to Ingrid, "I can't imagine getting rid of the wall plaque that my grandmother gave me when I was born." Ingrid asked him if he no longer liked it or if it was taking up space where he wanted to put something else or cluttering his wall. No, he said, he loved it. She told him, "Then that is definitely not clutter, and you just keep it where it is. But if you were tired of looking at it now, but it has meaning, then figure out a way to safely pack it and carefully put it away so that when you're married and have children, you might pass it on." The whole group of boys (who insisted that they weren't sentimental) loved that idea.

If you have room for stuff, and you love it and don't mind being caretaker of it, then it's not a problem. Enjoy it. But most houses don't have room for all that children want to keep. When stuff becomes intolerable clutter, the child has to learn to pick and choose.

Break the Saving/Keeping Habit

Brenda had enormous success when she asked her four children, one at a time, to help her sort through and get rid of her own clutter.

When she first asked her kids to volunteer, everyone made fun of the idea, but finally Maggie, her eight-year-old, offered to help. When Brenda finished weeding out a huge amount of clutter in her spare bedroom, she made a big fuss about how helpful Maggie had been, then took her out for lunch and bought her a new swimsuit.

Suddenly the other three were interested, and they all were helpful. She gave her oldest daughter the "privilege" of helping her with her closet because she was the oldest and knew the most about clothes and what looks good on Mom.

Brenda made it clear that it wasn't a job or a punishment; they could sit with cookies and soda and just cheer her on. She especially needed their encouragement to get rid of things that she had no use for and never wore but found hard to part with.

After she finished her decluttering campaign, she planned on asking her children if they wanted Brenda's help with their clutter, but she wanted to wait at least two weeks. Otherwise, she explained, she'd sound like the Wicked Witch of the West. "Hee, hee, hee, my little pretty. Now we're going to throw out all *your* precious treasures."

But she was surprised that within days, her teen daughter asked Brenda to go through her closet with her. When Brenda asked, "Who's next?" the others just went along with it—who knows why? Two of the girls helped each other.

Brenda recommends having the kids help you with your clutter, because it opens them up to getting rid of their own clutter. (Especially if you really ham it up about how much you love your ratty ol' ripped sneakers and then—with a look of total martyrdom—dramatically throw them in the trash bin.) If they simply cannot bring themselves to break their saving and keeping habit, then help them establish habits of *managing* their stuff. If your children keep losing something (or everything), then they need a place for everything and have to learn to put it in its place. Often this "place for everything" seems so simplistic. We've heard it all our lives, and we just roll our eyes when we hear it. But to children, it's not an old proverb—it may never have occurred to your child that certain things always go in a certain spot.

Another obstacle is if the "place for everything" is out of their reach—that shelf, that drawer, or that closet pole is just too high, or they don't know how to hang up clothes, or they never learned how to fold socks or other clothing so that it will fit into its certain place.

Sometimes children have sweet little tiny wastebaskets or clothes hampers in their rooms—but think about it: They don't have sweet little tiny stacks of dirty clothes, or sweet little tiny stacks of paper clutter. Get a great big basket for dirty clothes and a great big wastebasket. Maybe they need extra baskets for toys, games, or stuffed animals. If you or they think it will help, label the baskets and drawers till they get in the habit of putting things where they belong.

You can also help them find a place for those things that they can't let go of but have no earthly use for. One mom worked with her fifteen-year-old son, going through his jam-packed closet and dresser drawers. She'd always wondered why he wore the same four T-shirts all the time when he had so many clothes crammed everywhere. As they together sorted through his clothes, she discovered his Cub Scout uniform from when he was eight years old, his favorite T-shirts from junior high, and some gym outfits that were falling apart but his friends had signed their names on; and her son sheepishly told her he just could never get rid of them. Most of his closet and his drawers were filled with clothes he could not wear, but could not part with.

She didn't fight it. She helped him pack his treasures into a box that they stored in the attic. Now her son had plenty of room in his closet and chest of drawers, and could see that he had other things to wear besides the same four T-shirts. It was also a lot easier for him to put away his clean laundry, now that there was room to fit things in and close the drawers. It sounds simple, but often our children need our guidance to figure out these brilliant solutions.

Undertake Some Action—Don't Leave Things in a Heap

Ten-year-old Terry lost his glasses, and his parents called all his friends, asking everyone to search for them. Terry's friend David promised to clean his room to look for the glasses, found them, and didn't remember to tell Terry till three weeks later. Everyone, including David's parents, was furious with him. When his folks checked his room, they discovered that when David sorted through his clutter, he accumulated and stacked in a corner a huge number of things (including Terry's glasses) that belonged to other people, but never did a thing about it.

David had sorted out all his clutter, but he didn't take any action to deliver it. He procrastinated and left everything that had to be delivered in a big heap, where it was likely to start flowing all over the room and become clutter again. What a ridiculous waste of time! But he didn't know any better; nobody ever taught him that after sorting, you have to deliver everything to where or to whom it belongs.

Get Rid of It

Several parents have started a tradition with their children of once or twice a year selecting toys and books that they no longer use and delivering them to a homeless shelter or other favorite charity. Some families have children give one toy away to the poor or needy for every new toy they get. Many charities have resale shops you can deliver to, or will call every six weeks when a driver is in the area and offer to pick up whatever is being donated.

Once Ruth's family had started to declutter, every six weeks, when the Disabled Veterans called to say their truck would be in the area, she would just put up a note in her kitchen, letting the family know. It became a habit for all the kids to then look through their closets, toy boxes, and bedrooms and put donations into a bag. She doesn't even have to nag them to do it; they seem to be glad to do it because they know that their unused things will be going to people who need and appreciate them. If they have stuff to get rid of between the times when the truck is coming, Ruth keeps a big black plastic bag in the broom closet where everyone can put things to be donated.

Don't use a charity collection as a way to get rid of junk. Jack, who is a member of the Salvation Army, emphasizes that the poor deserve dignity. Don't send them clothes that are ripped or dirty, or toys and books that are too broken or shabby to be usable. Maureen makes certain all puzzles and toys with parts are complete, then puts the puzzle pieces or toy parts in a resealable plastic bag and seals it shut.

Heather has a ritual with her two preschoolers. Together they select the toys to be donated to the poor. Heather says that this wording is very important. They are not "throwing out or getting rid of toys," they are "donating them to the poor and homeless." Then they make sure all the parts and pieces are together. Next she spreads an old shower curtain on the floor in front of the sink and lays out towels on the floor, and together she and the two little ones wash and rinse each plastic toy. They put them on the towels to drain, and they dry them off and pack them up.

Heather says, "We spend a whole afternoon two or three times a year doing this, and there are so many benefits to that investment of time. We eliminate excess toys, so their rooms stay neater. Plus by the time I mop up all the water, the floor is nice and clean; but most of all, I hope my children are de-

veloping a sense of caring and giving to those who are less fortunate than we are."

Stop Bringing in More Clutter That Starts It All Again

As we brainstorm and problem-solve ways to get rid of clutter, we need to remind children that one way to get rid of it is to slow down bringing clutter into their lives, and one way to do *that* is to cut back on shopping and buying more things. Children need to be taught limits.

For children of preschool and primary grade age, you teach limits such as, You can't beat up on other kids, and You can't have everything you want.

For children in middle school: Follow school rules, and You can't have everything you want. Teens might be learning the limits involved with rules of the road and curfew, and that you can't have everything you want. Once they learn that the limits you are teaching are real rules, they often can accept them and live with them. Therefore, one limit children of any age can learn is that you cannot control clutter if you keep bringing more in, so *stop accumulating more clutter.*

If your child wants to purchase something that is clearly not a necessity, or which that child already has in abundance and has no more room for, then start the habit of having that child decide:

- Since I don't have room for this in my room or closet, where will I put it?
- If I bring this home, can I get rid of something to make room for it?
- Do I really need one more thing to add to the clutter in my life?

These are not questions to put off till after the purchase; they must be struggled with before buying anything that might add to the clutter situation. If you ask these questions with each unnecessary purchase, your child will eventually develop this habit of evaluating each purchase before making it. Don't you wish someone had taught you that lesson when you were young?

And here's a question for adults: If at a time that money is tight and you don't have any extra to put away for a college fund or a retirement plan, and if there is no room for all the clutter in this child's life, does it make sense to buy that child something he or she doesn't even need? What does that teach the child?

BENEFITS OF PROBLEM-SOLVING

Stephanie, the mother of three girls, said that when it came to decluttering, the hardest part for each girl was getting rid of things. Stephanie knew her softhearted daughters could never throw anything away, especially old clothes, dolls, CDs, posters, and stuffed animals, so several times a year they'd all problem-solve different ways that they could move their present clutter out of their lives.

Stephanie said that in addition to helping the girls move excess stuff out of their lives, these problem-solving sessions have had a great payoff now that the two oldest are in their teens. Practicing the act of problem-solving has given them an attitude that most problems are solvable. Often when friends from school are over, they'll be talking about problems that are going to "absolutely ruin" their lives, and Stephanie frequently observes that her girls will start talking in terms of "Let's do some creative problem-solving" instead of getting into the "It's the end of the world" mentality.

Stephanie said, "When my daughter's best friend, Riley, told us her parents were divorcing and she was devastated that her dad won't be living with them, my daughter suggested problem-solving ways that Riley could still stay close to her dad. Riley thought of some really creative ideas, and they work. Both Riley and her dad are committed to trying several of the ideas, because they cherish and want to preserve their close relationship. My girls tend to look at problems as challenges to be solved, not as something that will devastate them. This is not a bad skill to teach kids when they are young!"

PAPER CLUTTER

A generation ago, paper clutter was not a big issue for children. Times have changed. It's incredible, the amount of paper in our lives these days. Most children have the usual books and coloring books, and in addition they are swamped with announcements, flyers, old tests, school newspapers, notebooks, catalogs, lists of rules, and permission slips; they even subscribe to magazines. Children have paper clutter in their rooms, in their desks at home and at school, in their lockers, and in their backpacks. And now even little ones are in day care or spend a few days per week in preschool, so they are bringing home their art and written work and have papers cluttering up their lives, too.

Children are often as bewildered about what to do with paper clutter as we are. They need your help because sometimes they think they are *supposed* to hang on to all these papers. They need a strategy. It's time to once again turn to the Clutter BUGS.

Break the Saving/Keeping Habit

So let's start with reminding them that there just are too many papers coming into our lives, and nobody could or should try to keep all—or even most—of them. Demonstrate for them how much paper comes into your life and how you have to get rid of it immediately, or it will take over your house and your life. (Aha—even those of you who are not procrastinators are relating to this, aren't you?) The more control you gain over your paper clutter, the more lessons your child will pick up by your example without you teaching or saying anything.

Show them the amount of paper that comes your way,

both at home and at work. Share with them that some things are hard to get rid of—maybe catalogs or magazines—but that you know you have to. Talk to them if you decide to not renew a subscription because you can't keep up with reading all your magazines. They already know the word *prioritize*. Teach them that the only way to stay ahead of paper clutter is to constantly decide what to keep and what to get rid of, and this is a decision that must not be put off.

Twelve-year-old Corey was a "neatnik" who learned to manage her paper clutter several years ago, and kept everything—including herself—neat as could be. She told of feeling fairly burned-out a few months ago, and she just didn't want to make any more decisions. So she simply procrastinated with anything that came her way that needed any kind of deciding. Corey said she was in this funk only two weeks, but when she came out of it, the paper that had accumulated in her room, desk, and backpack looked as if it hadn't been sorted through in a year. "It was chaos everywhere," she said, "and it took me forever to sort through everything. Until I was done, I couldn't find anything I needed and was constantly shuffling through papers every time I wanted anything. I will *never* procrastinate about paper-type decisions again!"

Every time new paper comes into children's lives, they have to decide *now* what to toss, what to keep, and where to put it. And most of what they learn about their paper clutter also applies to E-mail clutter.

Undertake Some Action

As children sort through their paper clutter, they'll come across various books, magazines, notebooks, and papers that don't belong in their room. These shouldn't be plopped in a stack and set aside. If you do that, in the blink of an eye, the invisible paper clutter gremlin will sneak in, and all the neat stacks will merge with each other. Everything will be right back where it started, and all the time spent sorting will be wasted.

I believe there should be a sign hanging over every desk, in every bedroom, above every kitchen counter—every place where paper clutter accumulates—that says:

SIT AND SORT
STAND AND DELIVER

Teach your children by your example, by words, by whatever works, that right now they have to take every piece of paper in that stack of stuff that has to be brought someplace else and . . . they have to deliver it to where it belongs. Now.

Get Rid of It

Children, as well as adults, think of the wastebasket as an evil monster that gobbles up important papers. *No, no, no*—think of your wastebasket as a friend who needs to be fed. Supply your children with as many wastebaskets as they need and encourage them to feed their friend, the wastebasket.

When the time comes to attack their paper clutter, set them up with a big wastebasket or plastic bag to throw their papers in. Even better, become a recycling family and set up the recycling bin. If they have a hard time parting with old magazines and books, help your child play a part in selecting where to donate them. If they are reluctant to get rid of this year's school papers, then each year have them go through the few past years. It will get easier for them to throw away papers from years ago that they can't even remember.

At first, they will need your help to set boundaries on what papers to keep. Stanley, the father of four children, described his solution when his children made a big project. (And, he said, school projects are *never* small or neat; they are usually huge, awkward, bulky things that involve tons of paste, glitter, and coat hangers.) He would emphasize to his children that what you learned, doing the project or artistic creation, is more important than keeping the thing itself.

They would take photos of these big projects; each child had a three-ring notebook, so they put the photos in their notebooks. Maybe once in a while a copy of a photo went into the big family album, but usually the children were perfectly satisfied keeping the photos in their notebooks. Then, after the project stayed on display for an appropriate amount of time (usually until someone knocked it over or broke it), Stanley would discreetly discard it after everyone went to bed.

Select a Place for Everything

Howard taught his fourteen-year-old son the following clutter-busting principles: "Shuffling through the same papers over and over is one of the biggest time wasters and most frustrating activities known to humankind. Learn to *handle each piece of paper only once.* If you find yourself going through the same papers over and over, do something to stop it—put it where it belongs"

Sometimes a child seems messy and disorganized, but in reality, they just don't know where to put all their stuff. Help them decide where they can keep their papers. Would a three-ring binder work? Buy a hole punch and make it available to the children who are old enough to use it and not abuse it. Punch holes in the papers if there aren't any already. Put dividers in the notebook. Do they want to divide the book by subject or by year?

If the binders won't work, most offices receive paper in paper-size boxes. If you don't have access to these, ask your friends, and you're bound to find someone who will gladly give you boxes from her office that would otherwise have been thrown out. Or maybe large envelopes would be good for storing paper. Whatever you and your child decide on, it will have limits; it will be something that won't hold everything. When it's filled up, they can't put any more in it. This will give them great practice in the life skill of prioritizing; they can't keep it all, so they have to select just the most important papers to keep, and recycle the rest.

It will also be practice in setting boundaries. Every paper will not fit in the notebook. Will they need to set a specific boundary? If they bring home a lot of artwork, will they want to select just one paper a week or month? If they have lots of term papers, will they keep all of them or just a certain number?

Once these selections are made, the papers must be put into something where they will stay neat and the child can find them—otherwise, why keep them? And you're not finished yet. Now the child needs a place to put these binders or envelopes or boxes or files or containers. Where will they go? Top closet shelf? Bookshelf? Help them find a place to keep their books and coloring books. It's best to keep these in the children's rooms, because then when there is no more room for other things like toys or books, they will need to reevaluate and decide what stays and what they'll now have to get rid of. Again, if you run out of space, emphasize that they don't need more space, they need less stuff. This becomes a time to get rid of some or lots of stuff.

TIPS TO SHARE WITH YOUR CHILD

~~~~~

Clear out Paper Clutter in a **FLASH**
Feed your wastebasket.
Let go of papers (and old magazines, books, and
　　notebooks) that you don't need.
Act on it NOW—take it to where or to whom it
　　belongs.
Sit and Sort; Stand and Deliver
Handle each piece of paper only once.

If your children are discouraged and think that they are not capable of ever escaping their clutter, remind them of the story of the aeronautical engineers and the bumblebees. Also remind them that they deserve small rewards for small steps.

Now it's time to remind ourselves that we are all human, including our children, and sometimes all the great tips and techniques in the world won't help certain children. There are some kids who, no matter what, have just gotta clutter. If you gave it a good shot, and the child still happily wallows in clutter, well, at least you tried. Give yourself a pat on the back, and now it's time to reward yourself. Many parents find chocolate to be helpful at a time like this.

TEAMWORK

Ideas to Discuss

——Sit and sort; stand and deliver.

——Does your child have a collection? Does it still bring her joy? Is it taking up too much room and starting to annoy her?

——Would she like your help in deciding what to do with the collection?

——If she doesn't have room for all their stuff, she doesn't need more room, she needs less stuff.

——Do your children want your help in packing up to save or to give away to the needy or homeless?

——Do they want help in going through closets, drawers, notebooks, backpacks?

——Do they need a place or system to put or display their stuff?

——Do they want to be caretakers of all that stuff?

——If someone gives your child a gift that she hates, does she have to keep it?

——Do your children need help getting stuff ready to donate? (Does anything have to be washed, repaired, or packaged?)

——Can they cut down on bringing more stuff and clutter into their lives?

——Can you help them with brainstorming ideas for their clutter problem?

——Can you help them in selecting places for things?

——Feed that wastebasket.

——Do they want an album to keep photos of their art and science projects?

Ideas in Action

——Track down a place that could use your child's excess clothes, toys, and so on.

——Have ideas ready for where they can pack away, display, donate, or keep their papers and stuff.

——Ask them to help you sort through your closets or places of clutter.

——Make sure they have good-size wastebaskets, clothes hampers, etc.

9

~~~~~

If You're Busy and You Know It, Say "Enough!"

SOME CHILDREN BECOME SO OUTRAGEOUSLY busy that procrastination is inevitable. They truly have no time to do anything.

Since most young children have to depend on parents for rides to activities and for money to pay for everything they become involved with, their parents have enough control of the situation that they can either take charge and cut back, or tell the children that if they aren't able to start doing their homework (or whatever they need to do), they will have to drop out of one or more of their activities. It is usually the older children and teenagers who need to be taught to prioritize and to employ certain strategies in order to slow down their lives.

Children become overly involved to the point that they can't keep up with schoolwork or other aspects of life for a number of reasons:

- They are super achievers who succeed in everything they do, so they decide to do many things in order to succeed on a variety of levels.

- They are afraid of missing out on something, so they say yes to every opportunity that appears.
- They are trying to please their parents, family, or friends, or trying to gain acceptance, praise, or approval from someone, and the only way they know how is to become involved in everything.
- Their sense of self-worth is based on what they do and how busy they are doing it. (Have you ever received a Christmas letter that reflected this value in a family? You are meant to be impressed with how busy the children are.)
- They have just started to blast away procrastination, and they sometimes become superbusy just because they take delight in finally accomplishing something.
- They are trying to avoid something—doing home-work, being home, being bored, looking lazy, facing something in their lives.
- They have many talents and interests, and are pursuing all of them without giving it any thought.
- They are aware of what they are doing, but they believe that they can handle everything, even though they're dropping the ball now.
- They are following the example of some adult who does likewise (you, maybe?).

WHEN THERE IS NO JOY

Adults seldom have a clue as to how stressed children, even as young as preschoolers, can feel when they spend their days rushing from activity to activity. Extracurricular activities are definitely enriching, but when children are scheduled beyond their capabilities or beyond their comfort level, they feel tremendous anxiety. Also, they tend to interpret this style of living as "the more you do, the more lovable and acceptable you are." After this schedule becomes a habit, children can become obsessed with achieving, in order to feel "good enough," and no longer really enjoy any of it.

One clue or indication of whether children are scheduled beyond their comfort level: Do you detect any joy in their participation in their activities?

I believe children who become involved in sports, music, youth groups, and other activities are less likely to find time on their hands and therefore less likely to choose a path that leads them into trouble. Children participating in outside activities learn, grow, challenge themselves, and expand their horizons. And they also enjoy!

I certainly am not discouraging any of these involvements. Busy children are usually happy children. The difficulty occurs when you observe symptoms of procrastination, stress, or a perpetual look of sadness or frustration on the child's face. There could be many causes for this, and you need to take this sign seriously and to communicate with your child to find out the source of the problem.

Virginia noticed that her twelve-year-old son, Brent, was starting to procrastinate with everything—chores, homework, even returning phone calls to his friends. He was also becoming short-tempered; he was snapping at everyone, starting fights with his siblings, and being very cranky in general. Virginia thought the cause could be anything, and she started to worry: Could it be drugs? alcohol? a bad group of friends? growing pains? hormones?

One day, she and Brent were out alone together holiday shopping, and Virginia made some innocent comment to Brent about his bike in the garage. Brent barked at Virginia, "I *said* I'll do it later!" Instead of becoming angry, Virginia looked at him with astonishment. "Who are you, and what have you done with my adorable, lovable son?" she shot at him.

Her reaction startled him, and he quickly apologized, and said with a sigh, "I just don't know what's wrong with me." Virginia suggested they stop for pizza, and while they waited to be served, she asked what was up with him. Brent said he honestly didn't know and changed the subject, but as they chatted about the upcoming holidays and other topics, he started to open up and describe to Virginia how stressed out he felt. "Mom," he said, "I feel like a rubber band stretched to the max."

Virginia was astounded to hear these words from such a young boy. Although his problems wouldn't seem serious to most adults, the stress Brent felt was every bit as real to him as that felt by the staff in the cardiology unit where Virginia worked. The more Brent talked, the more obvious it was to Virginia that Brent was simply involved in too many extracurricular programs.

"Brent, there's no reason you can't drop some of those activities," Virginia said.

Brent replied, "Mom, I've made a commitment! People are counting on me. Mr. Johnson said I'm the only seventh-grader who does a good job taking photos at all the school activities. And the coach says he's counting on me to lead our team to the play-offs next year."

Virginia explained that just because Brent does a great job on something, that doesn't mean he's obliged to do it. Brent told his mom that he really didn't know how he got in this predicament, and she speculated that he probably got into this stress mess because of her example: "I think people like us say yes to everything partly because we want to be helpful, partly because it's an ego trip, partly because we fall for the manipulation of 'You're the only one who can do something,' and partly because we just don't know how to say no."

Brent could admit he was stressed out and that too many activities were the cause of that stress, but he wasn't willing to drop any activities. He felt it would make him look like a jerk, and if he quit basketball, it would hurt his chances to make the team in high school. He strongly defended his activities as his choice. Their nice relaxing chat was escalating into an argument, so Virginia dropped the subject.

During the following weeks nothing changed. Brent continued to procrastinate with chores and homework and snap at everyone in the house. Soon the whole family was feeling stressed. Virginia decided to take a tougher stand, and that same day her son brought home a test paper with an F grade that Virginia had to sign.

"Okay," she told Brent, "This has gone far enough. Sit down and make a list of every activity you are involved with. No procrastinating. Write it now." Brent could see that his easygoing mother was serious and on the brink of anger, so instead of arguing, he went to his room and started writing. Meantime, Virginia carefully decided what she was going to say.

When Brent brought her the list, she looked it over and said, "You're in basketball, Scouts, and way too many other things. You know I love that you are in Scouts, and have always supported that, and I know how important being in both sports and Scouts is to you. Now here's the deal. You can stay in everything as long as: number one, you stop procrastinating and get your homework and chores done, and number two, you stop being such a grouch. If you do not stop both of those immediately, you will have to quit *all* your activities, including sports, Scouts, everything.

"Frankly, Brent, I think most people with your schedule—

even adults—would be stressed and crabby and procrastinate. Now there is a third option. Instead of having to quit everything, you might be able to make those two changes by dropping some of your other commitments, which would relieve some of the stress."

By now, Brent was in tears, but this time Virginia wasn't willing to drop the subject. She went through the list with her son, and over the next few days she talked to him about prioritizing. As she had guessed, sports and Scouts were his top priority, but he still had many other commitments besides those two. Then Virginia talked about setting some limits on how to spend his time, and about how to tell the adults involved that he would no longer be working with their programs. Finally Brent agreed to try, and that same day omitted the most time-consuming activity—taking photos at every single school program.

Virginia was pleased, and then surprised when, a few weeks later, he decided to eliminate everything except his top two. And Virginia is delighted to report that her son's—and their family's—life has returned to the former peaceful easy-going rhythm that everybody enjoyed.

If procrastination is a problem because a child has too full a calendar, teach her some of the following concepts and techniques to help gain control of her life. If procrastination is not a problem, and the child is superbusy but doing fine, then this particular child probably thrives on and is happiest when she has an overflowing schedule. Just relax and enjoy it, and try to find some way to keep your sanity as you drive her to her activities all over creation. However, most overbooked children can benefit from some of these ideas.

Skills to Help Clear That Calendar

1. Be Selective; Prioritize

The first step is to help children understand how prioritizing works and why it's necessary. Your children may need coaching to determine what is important to them and to select the activities they want to continue, as well as what activities they can pass up for now.

Sometimes our children say yes to too many activities because they just don't know that they have a choice. They feel that if somebody has asked them if they were interested in doing something, then they'd better say yes. Sometimes they say yes because they want to do everything and don't understand the consequences of being too involved. (Many adults are still learning this lesson.) So they may need to hear—more than once—how hard it is to make choices, but that every so often we have to say no to some activities and decline some invitations. And that they have to keep at it until they reach a balance in life where they are involved in enough activities that life is interesting and challenging, but not so many that they are burning out or not able to function in other areas (such as school, which is the main "job" and top priority for most children).

When Beatrice started a conversation with her fourteen-year-old daughter, Annie, about her grades slipping, she presumed Annie would argue. So Beatrice planned to bring it up, then quickly drop it. "I'm just going to plant a few seeds," she said. Annie's after-school activities had increased to the point that she either wasn't home enough to do any homework, or when she was home, she was too exhausted to do anything.

Annie surprised her mother by saying, "You're right, but I don't know what to do." She told Beatrice of her frustration, especially that she thought joining the newspaper staff would mean writing an article every other month or so. But it had escalated, and now she was not only writing more, she was working on every aspect of the paper, and it was overwhelming her. She talked about all that was filling up her schedule, and how she felt she was struggling to find time to keep up with everything.

Unlike Brent, who was so resistant to dropping any of his extracurricular programs, Annie found that just hearing herself talk about it helped her to decide that she could eliminate several activities. Until her mother brought up the subject, Annie wasn't thinking of how to solve the problem; she was just hanging on by her fingernails, trying to survive.

2. Use a Calendar to Schedule "Days Off"

As your children grow older, they can use a calendar to keep track of their activities, and with that same calendar, they can learn to write in "days off." Some families call these catch-up days, where they have absolutely nothing scheduled. This gives your child time to regroup, catch up, or just veg out.

We all need some time like that occasionally. Lots of highly effective people believe we need "veg-out time" regularly; one fellow told me his style is to work like crazy most of the time, but then to take a semiregular "couch potato break" to recharge his battery.

In another family the rule is that if anyone, from the parents down to the youngest child, observes or feels that they are disconnected as a family, they'd request a family day. Everyone would vote on what to do, knowing that in this family of seven there is hardly anything that everyone agrees on, so the majority rules. Two things that all seven *did* love was biking on bike trails near the lake and sailing on their uncle's boat. However, both activities called for good weather, so they had a harder time coming up with family days during the winter months. Usually family day meant that everyone had to coordinate their calendars and cut back or omit something. They didn't omit responsibilities, such as a commitment to a church activity or band practice, but there always seemed to be something on everyone's calendar that was flexible and could be moved. These family days helped to recharge the batteries of everyone in this family.

Different children have different needs. Some need days off to veg out; others need days off to get together with family or friends; and others need days off just to catch up in general.

If you are encouraging or supporting your children to

shoot for something that really does take up all their time, such as preparing for the Olympics or something equally ambitious, no one is criticizing you. But realize that nobody can do everything, and your child will have to let a few things slide. That's not procrastination; that's another variation on prioritizing. There's nothing wrong with it as long as everyone involved knows that is the choice being made.

3. Set Limits

Most children need to be taught to set limits, especially the child who romps through life wanting to do *everything*. These children are usually very curious, often extremely bright, and sometimes multitalented. They want to see it all, try it all, taste it all, experience it all, and do it all. But children also need to learn to set limits when they are overbooked but haven't been able to get themselves to drop out of an activity or say no to someone inviting them to join an activity. Start telling them that, yes, they can do a lot in their lifetimes, but it doesn't have to all be done at once—today. Just because you *can* do something, or know how to do it, doesn't mean that you *have* to do it.

Let them know that you are not trying to put a ceiling on their dreams and goals. Cutting back and setting limits come up because their activities are getting out of hand, causing procrastination and preventing them from functioning properly.

Some children find all the concepts in this chapter especially hard. They think, "My band leader [or coach or teacher] will really be disappointed in me if I say no to that request, or if I drop out of that group." Some kids will tell you, "I cannot say no to this or quit this. It's too hard. I can't do it. It's not something I could ever do." They want to set these limits, but they actually feel incapable of doing it.

4. "Yes" Can Get You Overbooked; Learn to Say "No"

It is likely that your children will need your guidance to learn how to say no to an invitation or what to say when they want to discontinue an activity they enjoy. How do they say "I quit" to the person in charge, especially if that person is someone they admire or love?

This is a time to do some careful listening. As mentioned previously, parents often miss what the real problem is and are working to solve the wrong problem. For example, you might be nagging your child to quit swim team, and your child already has decided swimming is the activity that needs to be eliminated, but is terrified about how to quit or what to say. If you listen carefully, you won't be working on the wrong issue ("You must decide to quit swim team"), and you will be able to focus on the real problem ("Can I help you practice what to say to your swim coach when you tell him you're leaving the team?").

Practicing what to say is a wonderful way to work with your child on many levels. First, you can suggest what to include when the child first approaches the coach or the adult in charge. For example, the child can mention how much he loves being part of this program and how sorry he is to leave it, but he's overbooked and has to eliminate some things from his schedule. Your child can work with you on what to cover in this conversation.

Second, you can actually role-play with your child. You can play the child's part and demonstrate to him what to say. Or you can play the adult's part, letting your child practice his "speech" over and over. These skills will be useful to your child now, as well as in the future whenever he dreads doing something scary or intimidating.

Last, but just as important, this concept of assertiveness is the same one you can advocate when you talk to your children about saying no to cigarettes, alcohol, drugs, or other detrimental activities where it's hard to stand up to peer pressure. Even though most parents dread these talks and hope that school will cover these subjects, you wouldn't even think of procrastinating about these important talks with your children, would you?

As you help your child blast away procrastination, you will witness miracles. One of the most touching is to watch your child grow in confidence and self-esteem. When anticrastinators realize that they are capable of doing what they said they'd do, and finishing what they have started, they begin to feel enormous joy and ambition. But this won't last unless they learn to set limits, to pick and choose carefully, to say yes to some and no to others, and to slow down occasionally.

As children stop procrastinating, their self-esteem soars, they start to like themselves, and they feel exhilarated by their new ability to set goals and achieve them.

Tips to Share with Your Child

Help clear that **BUSY** *calendar.*
Be selective; prioritize your activities; choose your battles.
Use a calendar to block out "catch-up days."
Set limits; pause, breathe, slow down.
Yes can get you in trouble; learn to say no.

TEAMWORK

Ideas to Discuss

——Are your children feeling overscheduled?

——If they claim they are not too busy, ask them why they are not able to complete homework or chores.

——If they do feel too busy, tell them you have some great ideas that might help.

THE NEXT STEP

Ideas in Action

——Offer to role-play any difficult situations (such as dropping out of a group or saying no to a request from an authority figure).

——Decide how you will get this busy child to find time to communicate with you; maybe offer to drive to activities (so you can "car communicate"), write a note, or go out someplace, just the two of you.

——Watch your children for signs that they are or are not enjoying the activities they participate in; look for clues to whether they are overbooked.

10

Hope for the Future

AS A CHILD—A PROCRASTINATING CHILD—I believed I wasn't capable of returning a book to the library on time, so it was impossible to visualize myself doing anything beyond my little procrastinating world. When other kids said that they were going to go to college or become a doctor or travel the world, I didn't say anything, because I didn't believe that I'd ever do anything.

That's one of the evils of procrastination—it puts a lid on people's dreams and goals. But once that lid is removed, a world of possibilities opens up, and the lid can never be clamped back on as tightly as before. What an extraordinary gift to give a child—the gift of dreams and goals and hopes.

During a training seminar at work, Nathan and his coworkers heard a story from the book *Chicken Soup for the Soul* by Jack Canfield and Mark Victor Hansen. In it, adventurer and explorer John Goddard shared a list of goals he had written when he was fifteen. Goddard called it "My Life List," and it consisted of 127 fabulous mental and physical adventures. At the time the book was published, John Goddard (now an adult) had checked off 108 of those goals, including climbing some of the world's major mountains, becoming an Eagle Scout, exploring the Great Barrier Reef, reading the Bible from cover to cover, flying in a blimp, a hot air balloon, and a glider, and reading the complete works of Shakespeare.

Nathan and the others were then given the assignment to write a "life list" for themselves. It could be as long or as short as they liked, but the instructions were, "Forget about reality and just write the most outrageous, biggest goals that come to mind."

Nathan was interested in the fact that some people could scribble away, while others were stuck and couldn't write more than two or three things. Some people wrote of riding in spaceships, where others wrote goals that were so down-to-earth they were actually boring. He wondered what happens to make some people picture themselves achieving only everyday, mundane goals while others visualize flying through outer space. "Whatever it is that happens," he said, "I don't want to do that to my three daughters. I want my girls to feel free to reach for the stars, and I think one of the best things I can do is to help them learn to stop procrastinating."

Nathan shared this story with his daughters and encouraged them to make a "life list" several times during their lives. He told his daughters, "Look, I've set a bad example for you because I've been a world-champion procrastinator. But we're all going to work at blasting away our procrastination, and start reaching for the stars together." Nathan and his wife joined the girls in writing up a "life list" (it was Nathan's second one that week, but he didn't care). He was approaching this whole goal of conquering procrastination as a fun adventure, and he was determined to enjoy the ride.

Even World-Champion Eye Rollers Can Change

When Nathan would start talking to his daughters about rewards, excuses, or feeling overwhelmed, they would roll their eyes at each other and sigh, "Ohhhh Dad—" When their friends asked about the charts he had put up to remind the girls of their chores and listing their rewards, they would roll their eyes and say, "My dad's going through a phase. He'll get over it soon." But the more they teased him, the happier it made Nathan. He said that their teasing let him know what they did understand and what they didn't get.

One reward his daughters loved was Nathan going out with them for breakfast on Saturday mornings. They started turning around their procrastination so successfully that Nathan found himself going out to Saturday breakfast five weeks in a row. So when he had to work one weekend, he announced that everybody had to go back to her procrastinating ways because he wouldn't be available for a reward breakfast this week. (The girls laughed.)

He liked the progress his family (including his wife and himself) was making in conquering procrastination. He also loved the new level of friendship and communication growing among all of his family. The girls felt better about themselves, and he liked the fact that they were starting to believe that they could accomplish great things someday. His eight-year-old now wants to be a doctor. A year ago she would cry because when asked to clean her room, she didn't know where to start. Now she considers herself to be a capable person. (By the way, he says her room looks 100 percent better these days.)

I've warned him not to expect miracles and to remember that we all backslide now and then. He understands but says he can't imagine anyone—not him or his wife or the girls—going back to being the extreme procrastinators that they once were.

ARE YOU PROCRASTINATING ABOUT TACKLING YOUR CHILD'S PROCRASTINATION?

Some parents put off addressing their child's procrastination, hoping instead that the child will grow out of it, or find a way to stop on his own. If you've come this far and haven't tried to share any of this with your child, that's okay. Stop beating yourself up. Maybe this just isn't the right time. However, parents who hesitate discussing these concepts with their children often discover that a fear is holding them back. And once they identify the fear that holds this power over them, that fear evaporates.

Ask yourself—are you

- afraid of failure? ("This might work for other parents and kids, but it won't work in my house.")
- afraid of being less than perfect, or selecting an imperfect time, or speaking imperfect words? ("What if my child is in a bad mood when I start the conversation?")
- afraid of the unknown? ("I'm worried because I don't know what the reaction will be, what my child might say, or even what I will say.")

- afraid of being rejected? ("They do that enough. Why am I asking for more rejection?")
- afraid of making the wrong decision? ("What if I suggest something that doesn't work out for my child?")
- afraid of feelings? ("I might feel embarrassed, stupid, or inadequate.")

Identifying your fears isn't easy. Here's another way to approach it. Think about what if that-which-you-fear comes true. Then "balloon" that and see if you'd survive it.

- What if you teach them some of these ideas, and they don't work? You'd survive, wouldn't you? You might feel crummy for a while, but you wouldn't die.
- What if you were less than perfect? What if you picked the wrong time to talk to that child or used the wrong words? Maybe you'll start and get interrupted if it's the wrong time, or that child just can't pay attention because something else is happening. Or you might be the recipient of a teenage eye roll, or your child might say you're weird or crazy. It's happened before (hasn't it?), and you've survived (haven't you?).
- What if you venture into the unknown and something totally unexpected happens, like the child
  —blows up?
  —cries hysterically?
  —walks away?
  —ignores you?
  —laughs at you?
  —jumps up and down and has a tantrum?
- But it is just as likely that the child
  —looks you in the eye and listens

—agrees with you

—understands

—appreciates your doing this, although a teenager may not *show* that appreciation for a few ... um ... many years.

—feels cared about or loved

—likes the idea of working with you on this project

You don't have a crystal ball. You can't know what's going to happen. But whatever the reaction, you'll know you are doing something important, worthwhile, and caring for this child.

Maybe They'll Outgrow It? Not Likely

From my seminars and through a previous book on procrastination, I receive E-mails almost daily from adults all over the world who have changed their delaying ways and are now "recovering procrastinators." They share their joy and relief in overcoming their putting-off habit, but so many of them comment how different their childhood would have been if someone had taught them that there is a different, better way to live.

At the beginning of a seminar, Natasha handed me this letter:

> This is about *me* as a child:
>   I have always put off doing difficult tasks until the very last minute, even as a small child. In grade seven, as part of an enrichment program at school, I was asked to illustrate a story that myself and five of my classmates presented to the class (in the form of a slide show). I was very late starting these illustrations because I felt I would look foolish or let the group down

if my illustrations were not perfect. I became so distressed and so panicked that I took a handful of painkillers the evening before the deadline. I had to spend the night in the hospital because of it.

To this day, I procrastinate. Even a traumatic event like the one I related above was not enough to set me straight. I achieved well in school despite my bad habits and "laziness." Although I have achieved well "outwardly," I am filled with shame about my procrastination, which continues today (as I type this, I am supposed to be returning an overdue library video). I was a procrastinating child who turned into a procrastinating adult. This bad habit creates so much shame in my life that I now realize I must do something about it.

I now have two sons and I do not want to pass this habit to them. It has to end here.

Conversely, another mother named Estelle tried everything she could think of many years ago to help her teenage daughter stop procrastinating, but nothing worked. She said, "If all else fails, look at the long range—she'll eventually grow up and leave home, and you'll no longer have to fight that battle!"

Now she says, "I very specifically remember my daughter's bedroom looking so bad that I would just close the door . . . clothes everywhere, dirty glasses, CDs scattered. Well, this child is now twenty-six, married, with two young boys. Her house is always neat and tidy. It makes a mother proud!"

Some children do simply outgrow procrastination, but don't count on it. Most do not. And whether they do or not, do you want to continue living with that procrastination in your life now? Push yourself to do whatever you can to help your children out of that procrastination pit and to prevent them from living their lives with the shame, guilt, and anxiety of never doing anything on time.

Relax—You're Doing Fine

We can't measure prevention. If you give a child vitamins to prevent colds, and that child comes down with only one cold that year, there's no way to know how many colds that particular child would have caught without taking those vitamins. Similarly, trying to get a child to stop procrastinating is about preventing that behavior, yet we all know that everyone puts off things at one time or another, and so will your child. But no one knows how much your child might have procrastinated if you had not worked with her or him.

Maybe your efforts haven't stopped your child from procrastinating, but maybe you've opened up some lines of communication, or had some fun conversations, or started joking with each other. Regardless of whether you work on procrastination with your child, this book might bolster your courage to start other important conversations with your child or to say "I love you" to her. Even if you won't try any of the strategies from this book, you now have a better understanding of what's doing with your procrastinating child. When you realize that yours is not the only child in the world who puts things off, you may be able to be more patient and not go nuts when your child procrastinates. You may even start to see some humor in the situation.

One of my favorite stories of parents and children kidding about procrastination came from Victoria: "I'd been trying to get my boys (ages nine and eleven) to pick up the den for days (weeks). Well, one day while driving home from work, I hit a deer. I called the police from home to report it, and they said they'd be out in a while to assess the damage. I got off the phone and told the boys that the police were coming.

"The boys, who had not heard my conversation about the deer, jumped to the wrong conclusion. They had the den *and* kitchen clean in forty-five minutes! They kid about it now, when they have work to do . . . 'Too bad the police aren't coming today, Mom. Then we'd get it done quick.'

"I laugh with them, but since that day they know they can accomplish a lot in forty-five minutes, so now when it's time to clean up, much of their whining and arguing has disappeared, and they just dig in and do it."

Procrastination is the kind of topic that people like to joke about. Even though the consequences sometimes can be serious, there's no reason that you can't have some fun about it with your kids, if that's a comfortable thing for you to do. And if your children totally shut out everything you try from this book, then you can tell them, "Hey, even if you don't decide to stop procrastinating, at least you know I care about you." That's not a bad message for them to hear, even if it's said jokingly. You know how some people often say, "Like my father [or mother] always said . . . blah blah blah"? Well, what if some day your children say to your grandchildren, "Like my parents always said to me, at least you know I care about you." That wouldn't be so bad, would it?

Be proud of your efforts to have a deeper understanding of your children and help them stop procrastinating. Give yourself a pat on the back and . . . of course you know what comes next . . . *go get a reward for yourself.*

In fact, I think I'll join you. Hmmmm, wonder if there's any chocolate around this house.

TEAMWORK

Ideas to Discuss
——Go tell that child that you love her or him. Then give
    that child a hug.

THE NEXT STEP

Ideas in Action
——Reward yourself. You deserve it.
——Keep your sense of humor.

Index